MEDIEVAL
MONARCHS

MEDIEVAL MONARCHS

Series editor:
Elizabeth Hallam

Edward III grants Aquitaine to his son, the Black Prince.

CRESCENT BOOKS
NEW YORK • AVENEL, NEW JERSEY

CLB 4415
© 1996 CLB Publishing, Godalming, Surrey, England
All rights reserved

This 1996 edition published by Crescent Books, distributed by
Random House Value Publishing, Inc.
40 Engelhard Avenue, Avenel, New Jersey 07001

Random House
New York • Toronto • London • Sydney • Auckland

A CIP catalog record for this book is available from the
Library of Congress.

Printed and bound in Spain by Graficas Estella

ISBN 0-517-14082-0

8 7 6 5 4 3 2 1

Contents

Introduction

Medieval Monarchs starts with William I, the Conqueror, duke of Normandy, who invaded England in 1066 at the head of his northern French forces, subdued the native English and ruled over them for more than 20 years. It ends with Richard III who reigned for only three years, and whose death at Bosworth Field in 1485 brought Plantagenet rule to an end.

Excluding Edward V, the elder of the princes in the Tower, who was king in name from April to June 1483, 15 monarchs ruled England in the intervening years, their personalities imprinted, for better or worse, on English history. Henry II, who ruled in France as duke of Normandy, duke of Aquitaine and count of Anjou before his accession to the English throne in 1154, brought peace and prosperity to his kingdom. The first Plantagenet king, he was succeeded by two of his sons: Richard I, an absent king whose zeal for crusading cost his country dear, and John, sometimes nicknamed 'Lackland' who lost to the French king all the vast Plantagenet dominions in France, except Gascony. His son, Henry III, reigned for more than 50 years; his lasting memorial is Westminster Abbey, which he rebuilt in honour of St Edward the Confessor.

Two of the kings were deposed. The idle and decadent Edward II was the first. His extravagance and incompetence so disgusted his subjects that his wife, Isabella of France, found widespread support when she invaded England in 1326. The second, Richard II, was deposed by his cousin Henry Bolingbroke, later Henry IV, when his political ineptitude aroused bitter opposition.

One king attained almost legendary status during his lifetime: Henry V, who regained many English possessions in France. Edward IV, too, was a strong and charismatic ruler who earned respect at home and abroad.

Medieval Monarchs tells the story of these men, and their consorts, highlighting events and developments in their reigns. A short quotation by a contemporary writer introduces each king, and photographs and manuscript illustrations bring the times in which they lived vividly to life.

Rhuddlan Castle, one of the fortresses Edward I built to subdue the Welsh.

William I

THE CONQUEROR

(c.1028-87)

KING OF ENGLAND 1066-87
DUKE OF NORMANDY

'... a very wise man, very powerful, and more
worthy and stronger than any of his predecessors'
The Anglo-Saxon Chronicle

William I receives the allegiance of one of his subjects. The first Norman ruler of England, the Conqueror is an almost legendary figure in English history.

A Norman King

William I, the Conqueror, was crowned king of England on Christmas Day 1066, ten weeks after defeating Harold Godwinson, earl of Wessex, at the battle of Hastings. The illegitimate son of Robert, duke of Normandy, he had succeeded his father when he was only seven. While still in his teens he had to defend his dukedom against both ambitious neighbours and internal challengers. His success in maintaining his position no doubt taught him to manage his men, his government and his resources. But, as with all strong leaders of this time, it was the compelling personality of the man himself – his forcefulness, his energy, and the confidence and determination he displayed at all times – that made him an almost legendary figure.

A strong, charismatic military leader, William inspired his men, never hesitating to lead them into battle. But, despite his successes in the field, he never over-reached himself and resisted the temptation to expand into Wales, Scotland and Ireland in costly and debilitating campaigns.

He stands out as a forceful and able statesman in an age of petty wars, shifting loyalties and weak and confused governments. He quickly analysed those institutions (such as the judicial system) worth keeping in his new kingdom and those where change was necessary. Order was his watchword: he kept a strong hold over his potentially unruly barons, yet retained their loyalty, and taxed his subjects heavily, tying them to the land.

William was a genuinely religious and practical man who believed that the Anglo-Saxon Church and monastic system required thorough reform. He deposed Stigand, Edward the Confessor's archbishop of Canterbury, in favour of the learned and efficient Lanfranc, who in turn replaced the English abbots and bishops with Normans. Twenty years after the Conquest there was only one English abbot, Wulfstan of Worcester, and many English saints had been removed from the calendars of the Church.

The Normans also found Anglo-Saxon church buildings inadequate and unimpressive. A vast rebuilding programme got under way, and in a single generation a new style of ecclesiastical architecture was imposed throughout the country. The size of the major cathedrals begun after the Conquest surpassed anything already built in Normandy. The money came from the substantial Church lands now held by new bishops, while lesser nobles often financed the reconstruction of smaller churches, in order to ensure their personal salvation, and to impress one another and the king.

In an age of heavy eating and drinking and lax morality, William is remembered as abstemious and puritanical. Perhaps in reaction to his birth, he was absolutely faithful to his wife Matilda, the daughter of Baldwin V and, by a happy coincidence, a descendant of Alfred the Great, ninth-century king of the West Saxons.

William I hunting; he had a passion for the sport, and created the New Forest and expanded others.

William I's seal shows the king holding a sword; a strong ruler, he had learnt how to manage men when he was a boy.

The Battle of Hastings

The first and most decisive battle of the Norman Conquest of England was fought at Senlac, later called Battle, in Sussex on October 14, 1066.

Edward the Confessor (who died in 1065) had lived for 25 years in Normandy and ties with the duchy had grown increasingly close, especially towards the end of his reign, when the king spent less time on affairs of state and more on affairs of faith. Although Harold, a member of the powerful Godwinson family, had a strong claim to the throne, this was contested by William who, according to Norman sources, was promised the succession in 1051 or 1052. In addition, Harold had sworn in 1064 to uphold William's claim.

Depite these problems, Harold was crowned in Westminster Abbey on 6 January 1066, the day Edward was buried.

William protested that Harold had broken his earlier pledge to support him. When he got no answer, he began to prepare for invasion. He enlisted and trained an army attracted by the promise of good wages and a share in the spoils of victory, collected supplies, built a fleet and ensured that the Holy Roman Emperor and the pope would not be hostile.

At the end of August, Harold III Hardrada of Norway and Tostig, the English king's exiled brother, invaded in the north. Leaving some of his army in the south, Harold marched hastily to meet them. Before he could reach York, Hardrada and Tostig took the city on 20 September. Four days later, Harold surprised the resting Scandinavian army at Stamford Bridge and overwhelmed it; both Hardrada and Tostig were killed.

Unfavourable winds had penned William's fleet in the Somme estuary throughout September but on the 27th of the month they changed and the ships sailed for England. The English shore was unguarded, and early the next morning the Normans landed at Pevensey.

Harold heard of the invasion on 1 October in York. Thirteen days later, having returned to London, summoned new forces and marched on to Hastings, he faced William. William advanced to meet his enemy, forcing Harold to marshal his troops in a good but crowded position on a hill.

The English fought bravely, beating back the Norman infantry and archers. The hill was held through the day but fighting ended when Harold was killed, probably by a random arrow shot by an unknown archer.

William now secured the ports of Romney and Dover, marched on Canterbury and received the submission of Winchester (where the treasury was) from Edith, Edward's widow. He then moved towards London. To isolate the city and compel its submission, he ravaged much of Surrey, north Hampshire, Berkshire and Oxfordshire. Edgar, the last of the line of West Saxon kings, met William at Berkhamsted and acknowledged defeat.

Over the next six years, William crushed the opposition of the English nobles; he built castles and called in English titles to noble estates and reassigned them on a feudal basis to his Norman followers. In 1085 he ordered a general survey of lands and their holders that resulted in *Domesday Book*.

An evocative photograph of the Sussex downs, the hinterland of the coast on which the battle of Hastings was fought in 1066.

In Burgo MALMESBERIE habet rex xx vi. masuras
hospitatas. 7 xx v. masuras in qb; st dom que n reddunt geld
plusqua uasta tra. Una quaq; haru masuraru redd. x. den
de gablo. hoc e simul. xl. iii. sol 7 vi. den. Sequtau reddtr
de feudo epi baiocs. e ibi dimidia masura uasta. que nullu
Abb malmesbie he. iii. mas 7 dimid. 7 foris burg. xx. cotcez
g geldas cu burgsib. Abb Glastingbiens he. ii. masur.
Eduuard. iii. masur. Radulf de mortem. i. 7 dmid. Duran
de glouuec. i. 7 dim. Willts de ow. i. hunfrid de insula i. Osb'n
gifard. i. Aluredd de Merleberge. dimid mas uasta. Goisfrid similr.
Toui. i. qra parte uni mas. Drogo. f. ponz. dimid. Uxor Edric. i.
Rog de berchelai. i. mas de firma regis. 7 Ernulf. i. simil de firma
regis qua incaute accep. he due nullu sequtau reddun.
Rex he una uasta masuram de tra qua Azor tenuit.

HIC ANNOTANTUR TENENTES TRAS IN WILTESCIRE.

R ex WILLELMUS.

.ii.	Eps Wintoniensis.	.xxvi.	Walscinus de Douai.
.iii.	Eps Sarisberiensis.	.xxvii.	Waleran uenator.
.iiii.	Eps Baiocensis.	.xxviii.	Willelm filius Widonis.
.v.	Eps Constantiensis.	.xxix.	Henricus de Fereres.
.vi.	Eps Lisiacensis.	.xl.	Ricard filius Gisleb.
.vii.	Abbatia Glastingberiens.	.xli.	Radulf de Mortemer.
.viii.	Abbatia Malmesberiens.	.xlii.	Robertus fili' Gerold.
.x.	Abbatia Westmonasterii.	.xliii.	Robertus fili' Rolf.
.x.	Abbatia Wintoniensis.	.xliiii.	Rogerius de Curcelle.
.xii.	Abbatia Creneburnens.	.xlv.	Rogerius de Berchelai.
.xiii.	Abbatissa Scefteberiens.	.xlvi.	Bernard panceuolt.
.xiii.	Abbatissa Wiltuniensis.	.xlvii.	Berenger Gifard.
.xiiii.	Abbatissa Wintoniensis.	.xlviii.	Osbernus Gifard.
.xv.	Abbatissa Romesiensis.	.xlix.	Drogo filius ponz.
.xvi.	Abbatissa Ambresberiens.	.l.	Hugo Lasne.
.xvii.	Ecta Beccensis.	.li.	Hugo filius baldrici.
.xviii.	radulf pbr de Wiltune.	.lii.	Hunfrid camerarius.
.xx.	Canonici Lisiacenses.	.liii.	Gunfrid maldurch.
.xx.	Comes Mortoniensis.	.liiii.	Aluredus de Ispania.
.xxi.	Comes Rogerius.	.lv.	Aiulfus uicecomes.
.xxii.	Comes Hugo.	.lvi.	Nigellus medicus.
.xxiii.	Comes Albericus.	.lvii.	Osbernus pbr.
.xxii.	Eduuard de Sarisberie.	.lvii.	Ricard puingiant.
.xxv.	Ernulf de Hesding.	.lviii.	Odbus marescal.
.xxvi.	Aluredus de Merleberth.	.lx.	Robertus flauus.
.xxvii.	Hunfridus de Insula.	.lxi.	Ricardus Sturmes.
.xxvii.	Milo crispin.	.lxii.	Arnald canud.
.xxviii.	Gislebertus de Breteuile.	.lxiii.	Iacc de Moretania.
.xxix.	Durand de Glouuecestre.	.lxiiii.	Gozelin Riuere.
.xxx.	Walterius Gifard.	.lxv.	Godescal.
.xxxi.	Willts de ow.	.lxvi.	Herman 7 alii seruientes regis.
.xxxii.	Willts de Braiose.	.lxvi.	Edo 7 alii taini regis.
.xxxiii.	Willts de Moiun.	.lxvii.	Herueus 7 alii ministri regis.
.xxv.	Willts de Faleise.		

Domesday Book

In 1085, William 'sent his men over all England into each shire' to investigate his subjects, their lands and wealth. *Domesday Book* thus enabled the king to record the estates of his barons as well as his own and to check that none had seized land unlawfully. *Domesday* was also a record of tax due from each landholder. The book's title is a nickname given to it by the native English, who equated its sentence with the day of Judgement.

At the time of the Conquest most people worked on the land. Life was hard, barely above subsistence level. The main crops were grain, grown as food for both men and animals and to make ale, the national drink. *Domesday Book* frequently refers to 'plough lands' and to 'ploughs', which were the essential agricultural tool. They were often shared, although some estates and some working men possessed their own ploughs and teams. Partly because every available field was cultivated, there were very few herds of animals, although pigs were numerous, as they could forage in woodland. Much of the country was covered by forest, marsh and fen, which were gradually being cleared.

Most people lived in villages in the centre of arable land. Some men were free and held their own land, but even they had to pay their lord a nominal rent and help bring in the harvest. Most people were villeins, the next class down: each villein had his own plough land – perhaps 20 or 30 acres – allocated in strips within the communal open fields, but had to work two or three days a week on the lord's land and pay him rent, often in produce. Shepherds, carpenters, stonemasons and other craftsmen had smaller plots and worked shorter hours on the lord's land. The bottom rank was landless serfs, compelled to spend all their time tilling the lord's estates and forbidden to leave their village. *Domesday Book* was the crowning glory of William's reign. He died less than two years after ordering the survey to be made, while campaigning against Philip I of France. He was either injured or overcome by exhaustion while leading his army through the burning town of Nantes. Six weeks later he died at the abbey of Saint-Gervais, near Rouen.

William II

RUFUS

(c. 1056-1100)

KING OF ENGLAND 1087-1100

'... he was to nearly all his people hateful,
and abominable to God'
The Anglo-Saxon Chronicle

William II, Rufus, from a 15th-century manuscript. A ruthless, rapacious ruler he was assassinated while hunting in the New Forest.

The Unpopular King

William II, the Conqueror's son and successor, was known as William Rufus because of his ruddy complexion. He was initially popular: his first act as king was to distribute part of the royal treasure to monasteries, churches and the poor 'for his father's soul' and in 1088 he received popular support when he put down a series of uprisings led by Odo, bishop of Bayeux and earl of Kent, which he swiftly overwhelmed. The king, who thanked his people for their support and made promises of good government, was never to be so popular again. As soon as the danger of rebellion had passed, he increased taxation and enforced royal privileges more strictly. Popular resentment grew. Only Lanfranc, archbishop of Canterbury, could control some of the king's excesses, and after the archbishop died in 1089 William's violence, impiety and disagreeable qualities became yet more evident.

The attempt to wrest Normandy from his brother Robert Curthose's control was a persistent obsession. He invaded in 1090, made peace a year later, invaded again in 1093 and finally acquired the duchy in 1096 in exchange for 100,000 silver marks which Robert needed to join the First Crusade. The taxes William imposed in England to raise this sum were so severe that the treasures of churches and monasteries were melted down, and contemporaries alleged that many men were made homeless.

In 1091 he campaigned against Malcolm III of Scotland and, throughout his reign, tried in vain to subdue the Welsh, until eventually he gave up and built a line of castles along the Welsh marches. The burden of yet more taxes, to pay for these campaigns, together with poor weather and meagre harvests, caused more suffering. He quarrelled with Anselm, Lanfranc's successor as archbishop of Canterbury, about the right of a king to invest bishops and control elections, exiling him in 1097.

William Rufus was killed while hunting in the New Forest on 2 August 1100, in circumstances that have never been clarified. Although it was accepted as an accident, his death was also interpreted as an act of God against a dangerously irreligious king. So too was the collapse of the tower of Winchester cathedral, shortly after the king's burial there.

The nave of Rochester Cathedral; the rebuilding programme, which brought a new style of architecture to England under William the Conqueror, continued during his son's reign.

Robert Curthose, duke of Normandy. Although he was William I's eldest son, the Conqueror made his younger brother heir to the throne of England.

Henricus Rex filius   conquestoris genuit

Henry I

(1068-1135)

KING OF ENGLAND 1100-35

'A good man he was, and there was much awe of him ...
Peace he made for man and beast'
The Anglo-Saxon Chronicle

The Judicial King

Henry I, youngest son of William the Conqueror, was in the hunting party in the New Forest when William Rufus died. One explanation of the assassination is that the future king arranged his brother's death because he was frustrating his (Henry's) plans to marry Eagdyth, daughter of Malcolm III of Scotland. Whether he took part in a conspiracy will never be known. But from his point of view his brother's death could not have come at a better time, nor in a better place. He rode straight to Winchester, claimed the royal treasury and three days later was crowned in Westminster Abbey.

Henry I followed the custom of his predecessors and immediately issued a charter announcing his intention of correcting the abuses of the previous reign: vacant sees were filled (though with men loyal to the king), and Anselm was recalled. In the same year, 1100, Henry's marriage to Matilda, the king of Scotland's daughter, and a descendant of the old English kings, won him popular support. A few weeks after the coronation, his elder brother Robert, duke of Normandy, returned to Normandy from the First Crusade ready to claim the English throne. He invaded England in 1101 but renounced his claim to the throne in return for Henry's Norman lands and a pension. But Henry remained determined to take Normandy by force, and on 28 September 1106, 40 years to the day after William the Conqueror's decisive victory at Hastings, he defeated Robert near Avranches in a pitched battle that lasted less than an hour. Robert was taken prisoner and died 28 years later, still in captivity.

Henry was now king of England and duke of Normandy. He quickly restored order, punishing rebel barons, razing castles and consolidating his father's system of government. His influence on continental politics increased. Alliances

Henry I dreams that the common people and clergy protest against his government. He was a relatively just if harsh ruler, who influenced the development of the English judicial system.

with a number of neighbouring states were formed, but his principal opponents – Louis VI of France and the counts of Flanders and Anjou, plus a number of Norman barons – were increasingly restive and there were continual wars and local battles. Finally, by 1120, peace and stability seemed to have arrived at last, and Henry was able to spend more time in England. But in that year Henry's only son was lost at sea along with a number of prominent courtiers.

Henry became increasingly concerned about the succession, and in 1127 made his barons and bishops swear their allegiance to his daughter, Matilda, widow of Holy Roman Emperor Henry V, as his heir. She was then married to Geoffrey Plantagenet, count of Anjou. The last years of the king's reign were relatively trouble-free.

Henry died in 1135 on a hunting trip near Lyons, as a result of lampreys, a dish forbidden by his doctors, and today he is remembered for laying the foundations of the royal administration and developing the English judicial system.

Falaise Castle in Normandy. Henry I became duke of Normandy when he defeated his brother Robert Curthose at a battle near Avranches in 1106.

Stephanus in Regem magnatum laude levat(ur)
proles p(er) legem ... post domnat(ur)

post morte regis henrica regula legis
substituit tota placuit p(er) pra remota

Stephen

(c. 1097-1154)

KING OF ENGLAND 1135-54

'... a mild man, gentle and good'
The Anglo-Saxon Chronicle

An Unkingly King

A contemporary chronicler described Stephen 'a good knight, but in all other respects a fool'. A stinging verdict that was perhaps over harsh. No one doubted Stephen's personal bravery. At the battle of Lincoln on 2 February, 1141, he fought on foot long after much of his army had fled, wearing out a battle-axe and a sword before being captured.

He was a chivalrous figure – courteous, affable, kind-hearted and generous, if somewhat ineffectual when it came to carrying through the schemes he had conceived with such enthusiasm. He could also be sly and shifty, and on many occasions showed a considerable lack of judgement. Stephen was the third son of Stephen, count of Blois and Chartres, who had acquired European notoriety by running away from Antioch during the First Crusade, and of Adela, the tough-minded daughter of William the Conqueror who sent her husband back to the Holy Land.

Young Stephen was dispatched to the court of his uncle Henry I and given extensive lands in Normandy and England which made him one of the wealthiest of the Anglo-Norman landholders. In 1126, along with many others, Stephen took an oath to accept the succession of Henry's daughter Matilda. However, on hearing of Henry's death on 1 December, 1135, he set in motion what seems to have been a premeditated and well-organized plan. He crossed to England, was accepted as king in London, gained possession of the treasury at Winchester, and was crowned on 22 December. A messenger then hurried to Normandy where the Norman barons, after hesitation, accepted him as duke. In this way, Stephen re-created Henry I's cross-Channel dominion. Early in 1136 his position seemed secure. His Easter court was attended by many of the major landholders, and even Matilda's half-brother, Earl Robert of Gloucester, had done homage. Matilda and her supporters had been able to occupy only parts of southern Normandy and there were isolated acts of defiance in the West Country. However, Stephen made many political blunders during his 19 years on the throne – a reign that was plagued by civil war, local disturbances and even a loss of control of the kingdom in 1141-42. Arresting Roger, bishop of Salisbury, and his nephews Alexander, bishop of Lincoln, and Nigel, bishop of Ely, was one that cost him the Church's support. And on occasions his sense of chivalry led him to make mistakes that astonished and dismayed his followers, as in 1139 when he had Matilda at his mercy but gave her safe-conduct to her brother's castle at Bristol. Because Matilda, as wife of Geoffrey Plantagenet, count of Anjou, had a secure base in Anjou and later in Normandy, Stephen had to deal with a combination of external and internal opposition the like of which none of his predecessors had faced. Many people concealed treacherous intent in their apparent loyalty to him. In the end, however, he simply lacked the dominant personality essential to successful 12th-century kingship.

Wigmore Castle, one of the Bigod family's holdings. Although Hugh Bigod was created first earl of Norfolk by Stephen, he later supported Matilda.

Stephen's seal shows him in knightly armour, astride his horse. Chivalrous and brave, he lacked political judgement to an extent that dismayed his supporters.

An Inflexible Woman

Matilda, Henry I's sole surviving legitimate child, was married to Holy Roman Emperor Henry V when only 11 years old. After his death in 1125, she returned to her father's court before being married in 1128 to Geoffrey Plantagenet, count of Anjou. It was a loveless marriage, for mutual political gain, and the couple produced three sons, including the future Henry II of England, then went their separate ways.

Matilda alienated all whom she ought to have wooed when she ruled England for a short period in 1141-42. During that brief episode of victory she refused to stand to greet her two chief supporters, her uncle, King David of Scotland, and her half-brother, Earl Robert of Gloucester, and greatly angered them. She also insisted on levying an unreasonably heavy tax from the citizens of London, and turned their loyalty and co-operation into hatred and resistance; she was forced to flee from the city.

Haughty, hard and inflexible, she was critized by contemporaries for her lack of feminine qualities. But she was handsome and brave, a powerful woman in an age dominated by men, and could inspire great loyalty in others.

Carving of a lion, from a church in Anjou. Henry I arranged the marriage of Matilda to Geoffrey Plantagenet, count of Anjou, for political gain.

Civil War

The war of succession between Stephen and Matilda began soon after he had seized the crown in 1135, with Matilda's uncle, David, King of Scotland, invading northern England on her behalf in 1138. Conflict deepened when Matilda herself landed at Arundel in 1139.

The war had its near-decisive moments. In 1141 Stephen was captured at the battle of Lincoln, only to be exchanged against Matilda's half-brother, Earl Robert of Gloucester, who was taken at Winchester in 1142. But it was mostly a struggle of attrition characterized by sieges and small military operations, with Matilda and her supporters entrenched in the West Country and Stephen unable to dislodge them. Matilda was normally on the defensive, occasionally desperately so, as when, in the depths of winter in 1142, with Stephen's army besieging her in Oxford Castle, she had to make a dramatic escape by walking in secret through enemy lines at the dead of night. From 1142 there was a stalemate which neither side came near to breaking.

England suffered the devastation typical of this kind of war. Contemporary chroniclers tell a grim story. In the West Country, for example, 'you could see villages with famous names standing solitary and almost empty'. They also tell of the construction of castles and of local tyranny.

Such conditions did not prevail everywhere; but the normally peaceful English countryside suffered the consequences of an unremitting struggle in which neither side could fully control its soldiers. Central government disintegrated, with taxes not collected in many regions and coins minted locally by barons. Power was assumed by local lords who were given earldoms by the contenders vying for their support.

Matilda left England early in 1148. Her son Henry of Anjou, later Henry II, to whom she had transferred her claim, kept up the fight.

Stephen had quarrelled with Theobald, archbishop of Canterbury, in 1147, and in 1150 the Church refused to confirm his son, Eustace, as his heir. By now, Henry had established his domination throughout the territories of Normandy, Anjou and Aquitaine and, as a result of this, and the steady support he enjoyed in England, allegiances had slowly drifted his way; by 1153, great barons like Earl Robert of Leicester were ostensibly on Stephen's side, but in practice had done secret deals with Henry.

They were increasingly reluctant to fight a decisive battle – whichever side won, a massive confiscation of property would undoubtedly follow. When Stephen and Henry finally faced each other across the Thames at Wallingford in 1153, there was general pressure on Stephen to acknowledge Henry as king of England.

Henry II

(1133-89)

KING OF ENGLAND 1154-89
DUKE OF NORMANDY AND AQUITAINE;
COUNT OF ANJOU

'He possessed remarkable prudence, constancy and
zeal for justice'
William of Newburgh

Henry II, England's first Plantagenet ruler. Stephen acknowledged him as his heir at Wallingford in 1153, and Henry succeeded to the throne when the king died in 1154.

The First Plantagenet King

The first of the Plantagenet kings, Henry II succeeded peacefully to the English kingdom after Stephen's death on 25 October 1154. He made a vivid and lasting impression on his contemporaries. He was tall, with broad shoulders and the strength and endurance to match. His dress was usually informal and his manner courteous and charming. His sense of humour was strong and his wit mordant, but his temper was unpredictable and he could be bitterly vindictive towards anyone who roused his anger. His violent rages were legendary. Nevertheless, Henry read regularly, had an excellent memory, and according to the chronicler Walter Map understood all the languages from the coast of France to the River of Jordan, although he normally spoke in French or Latin.

Henry's policy, on acceding to the throne, was to rule as if Stephen's reign had not existed. He regarded the kingdom as his legitimate inheritance through his mother Matilda from his grandfather Henry I and, therefore, set out to reclaim royal rights as they had been before 1135. Stephen's land grants were not respected, and royal lands and castles that had been taken over by barons were taken back by the king. Although this led at times to conflicts, all rebellions had been defeated by 1158.

The king took control over the Church and supervised appointments to bishoprics as his grandfather had done. The kingdom's chief ecclesiastic, Theobald, archbishop of Canterbury, was a long-standing Angevin supporter and there were no difficulties with the Church until his death in 1162 when the uncompromising Thomas Becket succeeded him as archbishop, leading to a six-year conflict between church and crown. Henry also made use of those of Stephen's followers who were willing to serve him. The early years of his rule laid the foundations of the peace, widespread prosperity and well-organized government that is associated with him.

Henry II and his wife, Eleanor of Aquitaine, portrayed in a stained-glass window in Poitiers Cathedral; they were married in 1152, two years before his accession to the English throne.

Henry II's seal showing him as a man of judgement as well as a man of action; contemporaries recorded his love of scholarly discourse.

A Remarkable Queen

Born in 1122, Eleanor, the eldest child and heiress of William X, duke of Aquitaine, was one of the most vivid and remarkable figures in 12th-century Europe. In 1137 she was married to the young Louis VII of France, over whom she soon exercised a profound personal and political influence. The union was barren until 1145 when her first daughter, Mary, was born. In 1147 Eleanor and Louis went on Crusade, but were almost estranged as a result of her flirtation (and perhaps worse) with her uncle, Raymond of Antioch.

After Eleanor and Louis had been reconciled by Pope Eugenius III in the course of their return to France, she bore a second daughter, Alice. Shortly afterwards she met Henry of Anjou, 11 years her junior, and immediately set her sights on him. When she and Louis were divorced in 1152, she returned to Poitiers and sent messengers to Henry saying she wished to marry him.

The origin of the liaison must have been formed in August of the previous year in Paris, when the two had met. Like his father, Geoffrey Plantagenet, Henry took on a woman several years his senior. Like him, he also acquired great prospects through his wife: in this case, the duchy of Aquitaine which was Eleanor's inheritance. At a stroke Henry, who had become duke of Normandy in 1150 and count of Anjou after his father's death in 1151, became far more powerful than his lord, King Louis.

Eleanor's influence on the artistic, literary and cultural life of the 12th century was as great as her impact on its politics. Brought up in her father's court in the sophisticated ways of the Languedoc, she had felt an exile among the uncouth Parisians, and surrounded herself with troubadours and ladies from the south. Her marriage to Henry allowed her to found her own literary court.

During the early years of the marriage, Eleanor was actively involved in the political life of Henry's domains and, until about 1161, was regent of England in his absences. After 1163, however, she was less in the public eye, and it may have been at this time that her resentment against Henry began to grow. Although he gave her full control of the duchy of Aquitaine in 1168, Eleanor's rancour against him did not diminish. A year later, when Richard, the future Richard I of England, was named as heir to the duchy, he became her constant companion and fellow conspirator against his father. The coronation of the 'young Henry' as king of England in 1170 gave Eleanor another useful focus for her schemes against her husband. In 1173, her plotting reached fruition and the 'Young King', Richard and Geoffrey all rebelled against their father and fled to Louis VII. Eleanor was imprisoned by her angry husband.

Henry kept her in close confinement in England, supervised by his most trusted men. With her spiritual advisers she was allowed to travel only the short distances between royal residences in the south of England.

In 1183, after the 'Young King's' death, she was released for a time to tour Aquitaine in order to counter a French claim to the duchy, and in the following year was allowed to come to court to see her daughter Matilda. In the last three years of Henry's reign, Eleanor began once more to plot against him. His death, in 1189, allowed her to assume powers far greater than before.

Poitiers Cathedral, where Eleanor's marriage to Henry was celebrated. She came to resent her husband and actively conspired against him with their sons.

Archbishop and Martyr

Thomas Becket was appointed archdeacon of Canterbury in 1154 and later that year, on the recommendation of Theobald, archbishop of Canterbury, Henry II made him Chancellor of England. For the next eight years Becket was totally absorbed in affairs of state and completely in the king's confidence, not least because he invariably tended to support the latter in his conflicts with the Church. This loyalty made Becket Henry II's ideal candidate for the archbishopric of Canterbury on the death of Theobald in 1161. The king was surprised and angered when Becket, his most trusted servant, resigned the chancellorship immediately after being elected archbishop and became his most formidable opponent.

The struggle between king and archbishop was fought out over judicial responsibility and, in particular, over Henry II's determination to limit the powers of the Church courts: he believed that their activities were beginning to undermine the legal powers he had inherited from earlier English kings. At Westminster in October 1163 Henry proposed that clerks (i.e. people in holy orders, and therefore connected with the Church) found guilty of criminal offences should be handed over to the secular authorities for punishment. Even

Thomas Becket crowns Henry the Young King, Henry II's heir. The archbishop, who had returned from exile in France, was murdered soon afterwards in Canterbury Cathedral.

b eatus   ch.   Vigni.

Thomas Becket leaves Henry II and Louis VII, the French king. Becket spent six years of exile in France, from 1164 to 1170.

Overleaf: Chinon. Henry II died here, deserted by his two surviving sons, Richard and John.

under considerable pressure from the king and after several changes of mind, Becket refused to consent to this demand – or to others which Henry presented in writing at a council meeting at Clarendon in January 1164.

The king was by now increasingly intent on his archbishop's submission. After a final stormy confrontation at another council of barons and bishops held at Northampton in the autumn, Becket escaped to France, where he appealed for protection to Pope Alexander III. For the next six years he waged a war of words against his monarch and his new advisers.

In 1170 a compromise was reached between king and archbishop: Becket could return to England, the confiscated property of the archbishopric would be returned, and Becket could re-crown the young king who had only weeks earlier been crowned by Roger de Pont L'Evêque, archbishop of York. Nothing was said about the council meeting at Clarendon. On 1 December 1170, Becket returned to England – and excommunicated the archbishop of York and the two bishops who had assisted at the young King Henry's coronation. When the news reached Henry in Normandy, he flew into a violent rage, and four of his knights travelled to Canterbury where, in the late afternoon of 29 December, the archbishop was assassinated in his own cathedral.

Becket dead was immeasurably more powerful than Becket alive. Within a few months many miracles were reported at his tomb; and less than three years after his death he was canonized by Pope Alexander III in February 1173.

During the following year Henry II did public penance at his old enemy's shrine – a shrine which rapidly became, and remained, one of medieval Christendom's principal pilgrimage centres.

A Warring Family

Henry II was denied the peaceful and honourable end to his reign which he so fully deserved, largely because of dissensions within his own family, dissensions reflected in a panel the king was said to have designed for his painted chamber in Winchester Castle. It showed an eagle and its four young offspring. One eaglet on the parent bird's back and two on its wings were tearing at its flesh; the fourth was sitting on its head waiting to peck out its eyes. Henry said that the picture portrayed him and his sons, who would never cease persecuting him until he died. The youngest, his favourite, would, he foretold, hurt him the most cruelly. Henry's eldest surviving son by Eleanor, Henry the Young King, was born in 1155; his second, Richard, in 1157; his third, Geoffrey, in 1158 and his last, John, in 1167. Following the example of the great French princes, who frequently divided their lands among their sons, Henry arranged for the Young King to take Normandy, England and Anjou, Richard to have the duchy of Aquitaine, his mother's lands; and Geoffrey to hold Brittany as the vassal of the Young King, who was crowned king of England in 1170. John was excluded from the equation and thereby acquired the nickname 'Lackland'.

In 1173, however, the young Henry rebelled against his father. With Eleanor's support, a plot against Henry II was hatched with Louis VII of France, to whom the three elder brothers fled. Many of Henry's barons on both sides of the Channel declared for the Young King, and it took all of Henry II's political, diplomatic and military skills to defeat this dangerous coalition in 1174.

Although the death of the Young King in 1183 removed a dangerous threat, the remaining sons were anxious to know what was going to happen. Henry kept his intentions secret.

Family relationships deteriorated from then on, and in 1188, two years after Geoffrey had died, Richard and Philip of France united against Henry II. In 1189 Philip and Richard together attacked Normandy. Henry at first put up a spirited defence but his phenomenal energy suddenly left him and he fell ill. Accompanied by only a few retainers, he left his army and retreated to Chinon, the heart of his Angevin lands, to die.

Philip and Richard overran Normandy and Maine and forced the sick king to travel to Ballan, where they compelled him to accept humiliating terms. Henry was to do homage to Philip for all his French lands, and place himself in his hands, while Richard was to inherit all the Plantagenet dominions, including England. Henry was carried back to Chinon in a litter where, the next day, he learnt that John, his favourite son, had deserted him. He became delirious and died the next day, 6 July.

The king's entourage made sure he was given a suitably regal funeral. His body was placed on an open bier and, wearing his regalia and with his face exposed, he was carried the ten miles to Fontevrault Abbey, the favourite monastery of Eleanor of Aquitaine. This resting-place was almost certainly chosen for him by his courtiers.

Plantagenet tombs in Fontevrault Abbey; Henry II was the first of the dynasty to be buried here.

Richard I

THE LIONHEART

(1157-99)

KING OF ENGLAND 1189-99

'A man dedicated to the work of Mars'
Ralph of Diceto

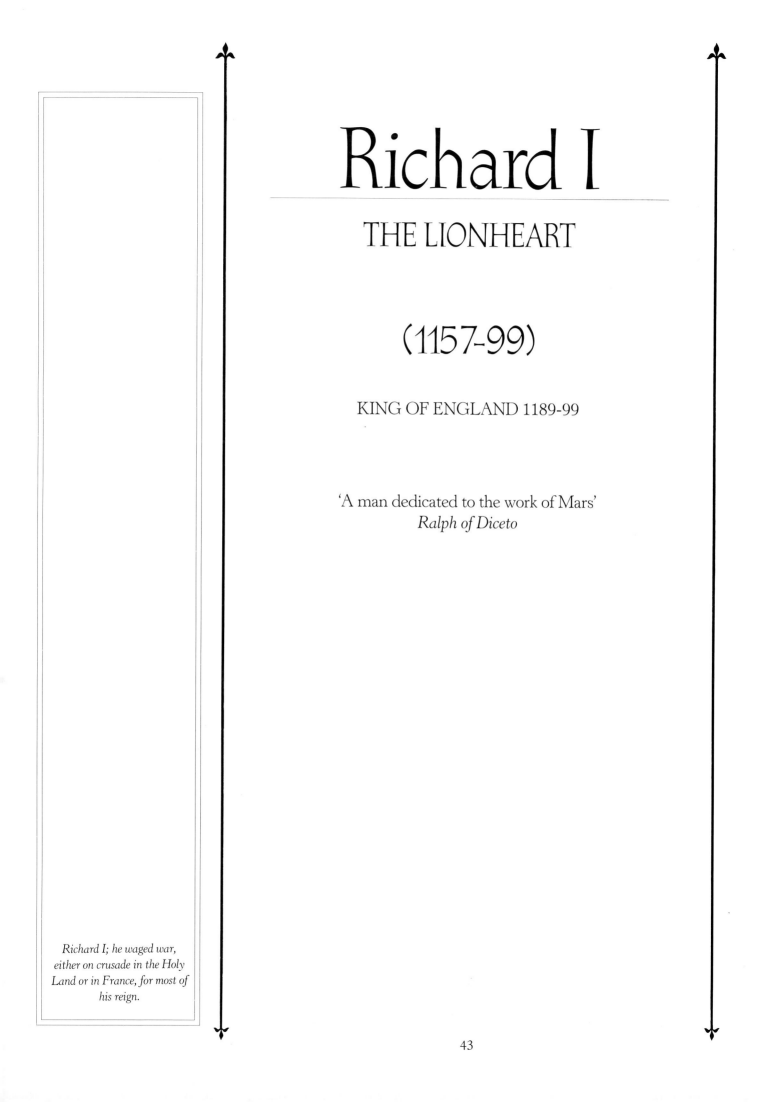

Richard I; he waged war, either on crusade in the Holy Land or in France, for most of his reign.

A Remarkable Ruler

It is not easy to distinguish the two Richard the Lionhearts, the Richard of legend, and the Richard of history: the legend seems to have evolved naturally from the real man.

Always the first to attack, the last to retreat, he was described by an enemy as the 'most remarkable ruler of his times'. A typical picture is of Richard wading ashore at Jaffa to relieve the hard-pressed Christian garrison, calling 'shame on him who lags behind'. Richard took the 'impregnable' Taillebourg in Saintonge in three days; and raised Château Gaillard within two years.

Reckless in skirmishes, he was once saved only by the bravery of William of Préaux who diverted the enemy by pretending to be Richard. In Cyprus, Richard told a clerk who dared to urge caution on him to stick to his writing 'and leave matters of chivalry to us'.

Less flatteringly, one historian describes him as 'a bad son, a bad husband, a selfish ruler, and a vicious man'. In 1172, invested as the duke of Aquitaine, he joined his brothers Henry the Young King and John in their rebellion against Henry II, even aligning himself with Louis VII of France. Although he fought for Henry against his brothers five years later in 1183, he turned against his father again, in 1188, and, with Philip II of France, defeated the English king in that year.

During the Third Crusade he cold-bloodedly slaughtered 2,700 Muslims at Acre in sight of Saladin's army and, on another occasion, at Andelys in France, he hurled three prisoners to their deaths from a rock and blinded 15 others. Selfish and violent, he once seized a valuable falcon in Sicily while threatening the owner with his sword; and became almost insanely angered when William of Barres bested him in a mock joust with canes. Richard was speaking what he believed to be the truth when he told the Holy Roman Emperor: 'I am born of a rank which recognizes no superior but God.'

He was undoubtedly a leader men could follow, just as his severity made him a king to be feared. When John's castellan of Mont St Michel heard that the king had returned to England after his captivity he dropped dead from fright.

Richard confessed his sins publicly on more than one occasion. At Messina in Sicily he threw himself almost naked before bishops to confess to the 'foulness of his past life'. A chronicler acidly commented: 'Happy is he who after repentance has not slipped back into sin.' The evidence for the recently fashionable view that he was a homosexual is slim; indeed, it suggests rather that he was a womanizer: he had a bastard son, Philip of Cognac.

Richard's generous spirit is shown in his forgiveness of both John for his treachery and plotting against him in his absence and, with less reason, of William of Barres for beating him in a mock tournament; and in his eventually giving the kiss of peace to St Hugh after the saint had first defied then shaken him. An educated man, he could joke in Latin at the expense of an archbishop of Canterbury, and while away the hours in his German prison writing songs.

Richard I's Queen

As a child Richard was betrothed to Alice, daughter of Louis VII of France and Philip II's sister, but in 1190 he rejected her for Berengaria, daughter of Sancho VI of Navarre. Little is known about Richard's queen, but it seems agreed that she was more prudent than beautiful and that the marriage was arranged for political reasons; it secured the English king a Spanish ally against the French. Eleanor, Richard's mother, took Berengaria to Richard while he was *en route* for the Holy Land and left her with him in Sicily in February 1191 even before Philip II had agreed to free Richard from his 20-year-old vow to marry Alice. It was Lent, a season when marriages could not take place, and Richard resolved to sail on for the Holy Land. But the ship containing Berengaria was separated from his main fleet in a storm and was found sheltering near Limassol in Cyprus. The plight of Berengaria, who was threatened by the island's ruler Isaac Comnenus, led Richard to attack Comnenus and to conquer Cyprus. The wedding of Richard and Berengaria then took place at Limassol, on 12 May 1191.

The marriage was a political success – for Berengaria's brother Sancho the Bold helped to defend Aquitaine against the French during Richard's captivity – but it was not happy. Richard spent little time with his wife, they had no children and Berengaria played no great political role. After Richard's death, she lived on at Le Mans where she was famed and respected for her generous almsgiving.

Berengaria's splendid effigy in l'Epau Abbey near Le Mans where she lived after Richard I's death in 1199.

The Absent King

The arrangements Richard made for the government of his Plantagenet dominions during his absence on the Third Crusade were practical. His subjects were already accustomed to an absentee ruler, for his father Henry had passed only a short time in each province. But on this occasion the distance involved meant that although Richard and his officials remained in touch through messengers, the king could only react to events at least two months after they had occurred.

Despite minor difficulties, inevitable in an age where the absence or illness of a monarch could pose severe problems, the arrangement generally worked well. The main threats to Richard came from his brother John, Raymond of Toulouse and Philip II of France – his arch-rival.

Crusaders depart for the Holy Land. Although Richard is best known for his crusading exploits, he accepted the responsibilities of kingship and made practical arrangements for the government of his lands during his absence.

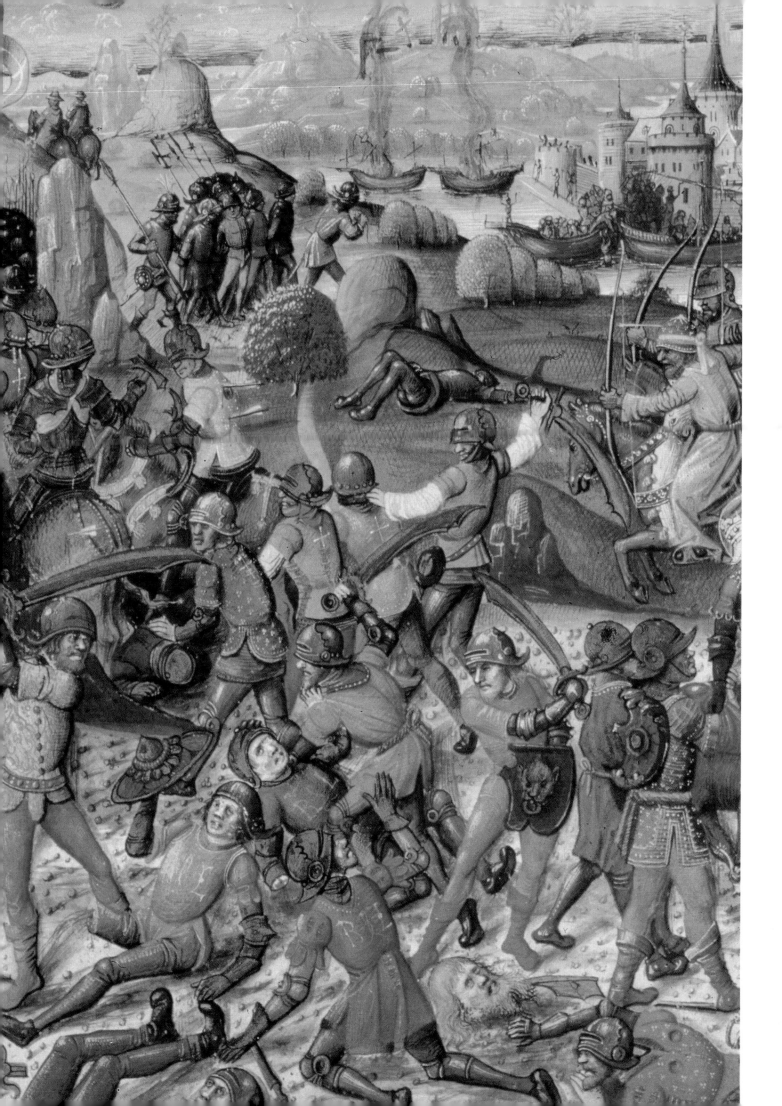

Crusader and Captive

The fall of Acre in 1191, one of the outstanding victories of the Third Crusade. The city remained in Christian hands until 1291 when it was retaken by the Saracens.

Richard took crusading vows in 1187 and in 1190, the year after his accession to the English throne, he set off for the Holy Land with Philip II of France. Most of the credit for the Third Crusade's success belongs to Richard, who was largely responsible for the capture of Acre in 1191. He also won an outstanding victory against Saladin, the legendary Muslim ruler, at Arsuf in that same year and nearly took Jerusalem twice – in December 1191 and June 1192.

The French king had returned to France in 1191, soon after Acre's fall, to intrigue with John and in 1192, after negotiating a truce with Saladin that allowed Christians access to Jerusalem's holy places, Richard set off for England. In December 1192, disguised as a kitchen servant turning a spit in an inn outside Vienna, he was captured by Leopold V, duke of Austria, who handed him over to Holy Roman Emperor Henry VI, an old adversary.

The emperor imprisoned Richard in Germany, at Durnstein and later in the castle at Trifels where he composed a song expressing the desolation of a prisoner and appealing urgently for his ransom to be paid: 'I have many friends,' he says bitterly, 'but their gifts are few.' He was released in 1194 only when he had paid a massive £60,000 ransom and agreed to recognize Henry VI as feudal overlord of England. According to later legend it was his minstrel who secured his deliverance. Blondel scoured Germany for his lord, and outside every castle wall sang verses which they had composed together until, one day, he heard the answering refrain.

It was apt that his rescuer should be a minstrel. Richard's grandfather, Duke William IX of Aquitaine, is famed as the first troubadour and there were close connections between the Plantagenets and these lyric poets, one of whom, the bellicose knight Bertran of Born, gave Richard the nickname 'Yea-and-Nay (*Oc-e-No*) – reflecting his sometimes treacherous changes of heart.

Jews are attacked by a soldier. Richard I's preparations for the Third Crusade caused hostility towards them and anti-Jewish riots accompanied his coronation in 1189.

A Wealthy Monarch

Contemporaries did not doubt that Richard was a wealthier monarch than Philip II of France. The biographer of Saladin and witness to the Third Crusade, Beha ed-Din, compared the two: Richard's 'kingdom and rank were inferior to those of the French king, but his wealth, reputation and valour were greater'. Other contemporaries drew the same conclusion. According to a chonicler from northeast France: 'in terms of land and money King Richard was richer than the king of France.'

These interpretations were probably correct. Philip ruled a compact kingdom which was far overshadowed by his rival's domains. Richard's possessions were broad and generally fertile. They contained many prosperous towns and sat astride the arteries of commerce: the North Sea, Channel and Atlantic routes and the lower courses of the three great rivers Seine, Loire, and Garonne.

Certainly, when Richard went on crusade in 1190 it was as a great and wealthy king. Although he had spent only a few months in England, he had used them well. In the words of a chronicler, 'he put up for sale everything he had: offices,

Château Gaillard, the lynchpin of Richard I's defences against the French kings. Richard boasted that he would hold the castle even were the walls made of butter, but Philip II finally took it from his brother John.

lordships, earldoms, sheriffdoms, castles, towns, lands, the lot'. Richard himself confessed: 'I would sell London itself if I could find a buyer.' In his absence, William Longchamp 'oppressed the people with heavy exactions' to finance his master's campaigns.

In spite of paying the £60,000 ransom to Henry VI – and this without Longchamp's skills to help – Richard was able to raise enough money between 1194 and 1199 to build the magnificent Château Gaillard and keep his dominions intact.

Richard's 'saucy castle' or 'castle of the rock', Château Gaillard was at the centre of the fortifications that protected Rouen, capital of his duchy of Normandy, against the French. A network of roads, bridges and forts radiated from this formidable fortress, with its concentric walls, rock-cut ditches and elliptical citadel whose curvilinear wall allowed the defenders' missiles to sweep any approach a besieger might take.

Richard's brainchild, the product of his mastery of siegecraft, the castle was distinguished by the hectic speed of its construction – a mere two years – and by the king's close personal interest in the design and building. That it was also distinguished by its cost – £11,500 was spent on the castle alone – is a tribute to Richard's ability to raise money.

The Lion's Death

In just ten years Richard earned a place in the history of England, France, Europe and the Crusades. His military achievements are widely acknowledged. He was skilled in siege warfare, in battle, and in castle-building, and England and his French lands were relatively well governed even in his absences. He will always be best remembered for his crusading exploits, when his courage and military skill earned him a reputation shared by no other English king.

Richard was killed, not in a major battle to defend his inheritance, but when besieging the castle of Chalus-Chabrol, held by the rebellious *vicomte* of Limoges. On 26 March 1199 the king was inspecting the progress made by his own troops, armed only with a helmet and shield. A lone crossbowman on the castle wall shot at him; Richard admired this brave gesture but was too late in getting out of the way. The bolt entered his shoulder, and was removed only with difficulty. Richard stayed in his tent to recuperate – but his wound turned gangrenous and the infection spread. His mother, Eleanor of Aquitaine, hastened to his bedside, but the powerful king's strength ebbed away, and on 7 April he died. His heart was buried in Rouen Cathedral, his entrails at Charroux in Poitou and his body, like that of his father, Henry II, was buried at Fontevrault Abbey, at the heart of his mighty Angevin dominions.

Fontevrault Abbey, mausoleum of the Plantagenet family. It contains the tombs of Richard I, Henry II, Eleanor of Aquitaine and John's wife, Isabella of Angoulême.

Richard I's effigy at Rouen; his heart is buried here, his entrails at Charroux in Poitou, and his body in Fontevrault Abbey.

John

(1167-1216)

KING OF ENGLAND (1199-1216)
LORD OF IRELAND

'Indeed a great prince, but scarcely a happy one'
Barnwell annalist

John, Richard I's younger brother and Henry II's favourite son, lost Plantagenet dominions to Philip II of France.

The King who Failed

John became king of England in 1199 on the death of his brother Richard I. Many contemporary writers emphasized his ruthlessness, cruelty, greed and lust. John's father, Henry II, had also been accused of these faults, but he was far more successful as a king. John's lack of more than momentary military success, from his first military expedition to Ireland in 1185 to his war against the rebel barons at the end of his reign, was a severe drawback in the eyes of his subjects.

Although many called him John 'Softsword', he was dilatory rather than cowardly. He had deserted his father Henry II in 1189, and, angered by Richard's choice of Arthur, duke of Britanny, as his heir, had intrigued against his brother during his absence on the Third Crusade, helped by Philip II of France. However, John retained the support of some important barons as well as families entirely dependent on him for their position, but many nobles and landholders did not trust him and he could maintain their allegiance only by taking hostages and keeping them in debt to him. He could be generous to people who could not harm him, but vicious to people in his power.

His quarrel with Pope Innocent III over Stephen Langton's appointment as archbishop of Canterbury in 1206 resulted in an interdict on England from 1208 to 1213 and cost him the support of some churchmen; he was himself excommunicated in 1212.

His reign was notable for the loss to Philip II of the great part of the vast Plantagenet dominions in France, despite the great victory he won at Mirebeau when he rescued his mother from the castle, under siege by Arthur and his French allies. He captured Arthur and Hugh of Lusignan, but later released the latter. His cruel treatment of Arthur, allegedly murdered at Rouen in 1203, and of his other prisoners alienated many of his remaining subjects in France, and in 1203–4 the French king was able to dispossess him of Normandy, Maine, Touraine, Anjou and Poitou with relative ease. Although John recovered Gascony and southern Poitou in 1205–6, his overall losses were immense.

On his return to England in 1211, he faced the threat of French invasion and ever-increasing hostility from his barons, who, further angered by costly and abortive expeditions in 1212 and 1213–14 to recover his French lands, forced him to agree, temporarily, to the terms of Magna Carta.

Silver pennies during John's reign showing the king's head.

The French Connection

Lusignan. Isabella of Angoulême, John's second wife, had been betrothed to Hugh the Brown, count of Lusignan, before her marriage to the English king, and married Hugh's son after John's death.

John's mother and his second wife, Isabella of Angoulême, whom he married after divorcing Isabella of Gloucester, were both influential in his relations with France. He was Eleanor's youngest child and, when Richard died in 1199, she supported him against her grandson, Arthur, duke of Brittany, and brought Richard's mercenary troops to his aid. She held her duchy of Aquitaine for John when Anjou, Maine and Touraine decided in favour of Arthur, and later that year made it over to him. In 1201, virtually bedridden, she used her remaining arts of persuasion on John's behalf in an attempt to calm the turbulent barons of Poitou.

Before her marriage to John, Isabella had been betrothed to Hugh, the Brown, count of Lusignan, and John confiscated Hugh's county in 1201, as a gift for Isabella's father Audemar. Hugh appealed for help to the peers of France at Paris, providing Philip II, the king's French overlord, with a pretext for pronouncing John's lands in France confiscated and giving legal validity to Philip's subsequent conquests.

The Great Charter

John's final humiliation in France when Philip II defeated his allies at the battle of Bouvines on 27 July 1214 was followed in 1215 by a further surrender of power at home when his rebellious barons forced him to seal Magna Carta at Runnymede. As a treaty of peace between the king and his barons it was not successful: the war it sought to prevent broke out after a few months. Some of its terms, such as removing John's administrators and returning his mercenary troops to the continent, were the result of temporary political circumstances and did not last. Most of the precepts were more permanent.

Magna Carta begins with a general guarantee of privileges to the Church and goes on to deal with the grievances of the baronage. The charter also protected from exploitation any heir who was under age when his father died and so fell into the king's wardship; it laid down that any widow should receive her marriage portion immediately on her husband's death and that she should be free to choose whether or not to remarry; and it prevented the unnecessary seizure of the lands of Jews or debtors to the king. The rights which the king granted to his barons were to be conceded by them to their tenants, so the charter's effects spread down from the upper levels of society. It also dealt with consent to taxation.

Provisions were made to ensure that the royal court was in a fixed place – in practice, Westminster – where the king's justice could always be obtained, and that royal judges would visit each county regularly. Restrictions were put on the powers of the king's local officials, particularly sheriffs. The extent of the king's forests was to be reduced and the powers of his forest justices limited. Clauses regulated weights and measures, ensured the safety of merchants and confirmed the privileges of the citizens of London.

Some terms of Magna Carta enunciated principles which have been a recurring theme in English history and have had a lasting signficance: the upholding of individual rights against arbitrary government.

John's defeat at the battle of Bouvines made him vulnerable to the baronial rebellion which led to his sealing Magna Carta.

The Great Charter; John was forced to agree to its terms in 1215, and it has been a cornerstone of English rights ever since.

ficoꝛ de tam inopinata victoria letuſ: gꝛaſ deo ex
ſoluit ꝗ ſibi talem ꝯceſſit ab aduſariuſ poꝛtaꝛe triũ
phũ. Treſ ꝗ comiteſ ſupꝺꝺm cũ militũ ⁊ alioꝛum
numioſa multitudĩe uinctiſ ꝯſtĩctĩ abducti ſunt:
carcerali cuſtodie mancĩpanꝺi. In aduentu aũ reg
tota ciuitaſ pariſiaca ſacleb; ⁊ latuiſ cantib; ⁊ plau
ſib; claſſiciſ ⁊ lauꝺib; ꝺiez ⁊ nocte ſeſquĩte ſericiſ ⁊ ua
riiſ oꝛnata pannIſ ſollenꝰ exultabat ſacta ⁊ aut
h belli ꝺgreſſio menſe iulio ⁊ĩ· kl· auguſtĩ——⁊·

ariũ

equ

ang

ꝺur

ꝺur

Steph

accep

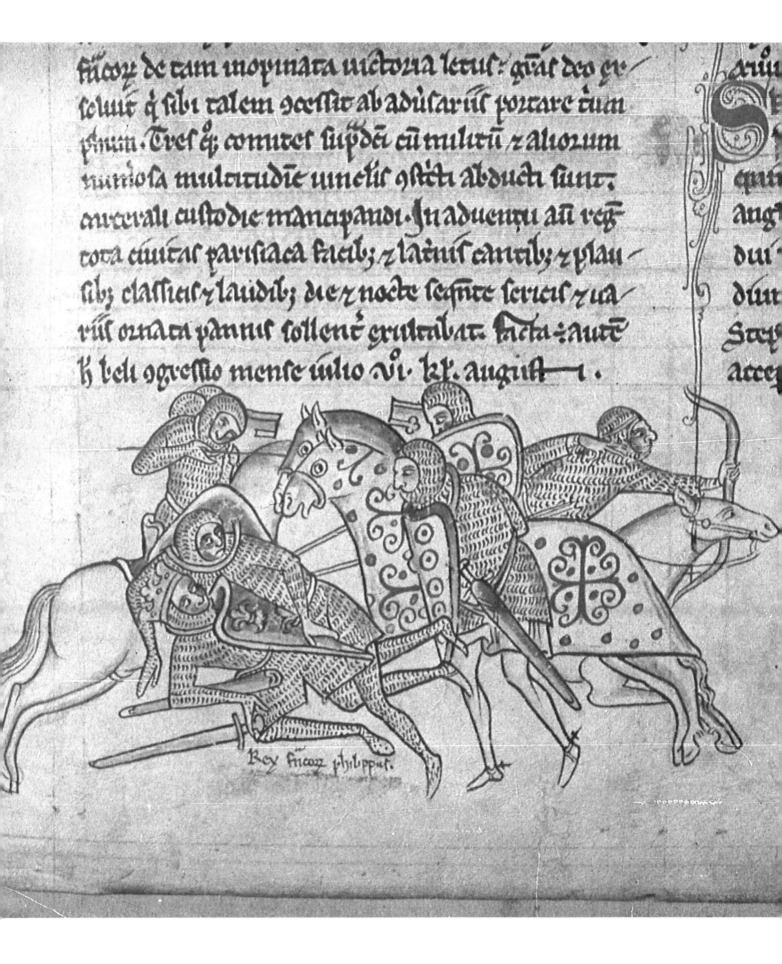

Rex ſrncoꝛ philippuſ.

Burial in England

The Wash where, according to legend, John lost all his baggage. A contemporary records that some members of his household were submerged in quicksand, together with packhorses and chapel goods.

Within five months of Magna Carta, war broke out between John and his barons once more and in May 1216, a year after he had set his seal to the charter, Prince Louis of France, son of Philip II, crossed to England to seize John's throne. This was at the invitation of a number of leading English barons, who were angry because John had shown no signs of keeping the promises he had made in the charter. By the end of the summer Louis was losing support, and John advanced from the West Midlands to help his beleaguered followers at Windsor. In September, he drove back Alexander I of Scotland, who had reached Cambridge, and temporarily relieved Lincoln. Soon afterwards he fell ill.

On 11 October John and his entourage tried to return from Norfolk to Lincolnshire by the quickest and shortest route, across the Wellstream estuary. However, they set out before the tide had receded and as a result, the king lost chapel goods, pack animals and some members of his household.

John, increasingly ill, pressed on to Newark in Nottinghamshire, where he was attended by a doctor, the abbot of Croxton. He died in Newark Castle on 19 October. Immediately, his household servants robbed him of his personal goods. His intestines were taken by the abbot and entombed at Croxton Abbey, but in accordance with his will his body was buried in Worcester Cathedral. Henry II and Richard I had been buried at Fontevrault in Anjou. John, who had lost the heartlands of the Plantagenet dominions, and had spent so much of his reign in his English kingdom, was appropriately buried in an English cathedral near an English saint.

John's effigy in Worcester Cathedral. He was the first Plantagenet king to be buried in England.

Henry III

(1207-72)

KING OF ENGLAND 1216-72

'In his lifetime he honoured St Edward the Confessor
and venerated him with special devotion'
Chronicle of Thomas Wykes

*Henry III; he was nine years
old when he became king, but
it was nearly 20 years before
his personal rule began.*

A Dutiful King

Henry III was described by a contemporary as being of medium height and strong build, with a drooping eyelid hiding part of the pupil.

No Plantagenet king had come to the throne in more difficult circumstances. When Henry's father John died, Louis, son of Philip II, king of France, controlled the whole of eastern England, including London, and was recognized as king by the majority of English barons. However, within a year, his regent, William Marshal, earl of Pembroke, had carried the Plantagenet standard to victory over Louis. Henry was undisputed king. William Marshal died in May 1219, but although Henry's minority was brought completely to an end in January 1227, he remained under the influence of great ministers inherited from his father until 1234. Only then did his personal rule begin.

For Henry, the duties of kingship were summed up in the oath he swore in 1220, which pledged him to maintain peace, dispense justice and uphold the rights of the crown.

Abroad, Henry was more ambitious, launching schemes to regain the Plantagenet lands in France (he invaded Brittany in 1230 and Poitou in 1242 – both fruitlessly) and, in the 1250s, to install his young son Edmund as king of Sicily. But he could raise neither adequate finances nor the support of his barons, which he needed for any effective action; and to most of his subjects, such unrealistic notions were further proof of his 'simplicity'. In England, Henry's political ineptitude provoked widespread hostility, and in 1258 a group of barons under the leadership of Simon de Montfort forced him to accept the Provisions of Oxford, an ambitious and wide-ranging programme of reform.

Henry temperamentally was more suited to the peaceful style of post-Magna Carta kingship. Not for him his father's hectic travelling and energetic government. In 1244, Matthew Paris noted that the king preferred the 'delight and rest' of his palace of Westminster to a campaign in Wales. Henry yearned for an easy life. He was indifferent to hunting and tournaments, antipathetic to the rigours of campaigns and soldiering. He liked to spend comfortable weeks, sometimes months, at his favourite palaces, within a few days' travelling distance of each other in the home counties: Westminster, Windsor, Winchester, Clarendon, Marlborough and (the furthest north) Woodstock.

Like all Plantagenets, Henry had a fierce temper. However, it was easily appeased and descriptions of his meetings with Matthew Paris show that he was accessible, affable, courteous and sympathetic. The king's piety brought him widespread respect. He gave alms on a grand scale – feeding 500 paupers every day in the 1240s – and also every day, was said to hear Mass four times. From 1245 onwards, he spent vast sums of money rebuilding Westminster Abbey in honour of his patron saint, Edward the Confessor.

His reign defined the position of the English monarchy until the end of the 15th century. It was a kingship limited by law, and in particular by the terms of Magna Carta. But it was not limited by anything more radical. The Provisions of Oxford had failed, and no legal restraints could be imposed on the king's ability to do what he liked in the vital areas of policy, patronage and appointments.

Henry III lands in Aquitaine. He styled himself duke of Normandy, duke of Aquitaine and count of Anjou, but had effective control only of Gascony.

William Marshal, earl of Pembroke. Regent for the young king from 1216 to 1219, he epitomized the chivalric virtues of gallantry and loyalty.

The Queen's Relations

Henry III married Eleanor, second daughter of the count of Provence, in 1236. The count's eldest daughter was the wife of Louis IX of France, and Henry doubtless hoped that this new connection with the king of France, his kinsman, would increase his continental influence. Fundamentally, however, Henry wanted to get married. He was in his late twenties, and his piety denied him the mistresses enjoyed by his Plantagenet predecessors.

There is no physical description of Eleanor, but since her son Edward was over six feet tall, it is conceivable that she was a good deal taller than her husband. Certainly, she eventually developed a far stronger and more determined personality than Henry.

Two of her uncles, members of the great princely house of Savoy, were brought to England by Henry, and in 1240 Peter of Savoy was granted the honour of Richmond; a year later his brother Boniface became archbishop of Canterbury.

In England, Peter and Boniface were accepted more easily than a second group of foreign relatives, the Lusignans. These were the king's half-brothers, the children of the second marriage of his mother, Isabella of Angoulême, to the great Poitevin prince, Hugh, lord of Lusignan. Henry made one of them, William de Valence, earl of Pembroke in 1247. Another, Aymer, became bishop-elect of Winchester. At the same time, Henry ensured that the sons of the earls of Gloucester and Derby, the young earls of Surrey and Devon, married into the Savoyard and Lusignan families. His aim was to bring his native barons into a harmonious family circle at court. However, he lacked the skill to succeed in this aim, and there were deep and damaging divisions between the two elements in his court.

Henry III and his queen, Eleanor of Provence. Their marriage was happy, but she and her relatives played a malign role in English politics.

Reform and Rebellion

In 1258 Henry III's policies produced a political revolution, followed by three years of savage civil war. His government had appointed sheriffs to raise large amounts of revenue. Knights, gentry and their followers naturally suffered. They were also oppressed by the barons, who, in their turn, could not ignore the grievances of these lesser men.

As a result, a programme of reform was produced that was far more radical and wide-ranging than any seen in England before or since: the Provisions of Oxford (followed by the Provisions of Westminster in 1259). A council of 15 was imposed on Henry III, who could not govern without its consent.

One of the members of the council was Simon de Montfort, who had inherited the English earldom of Leicester through his mother and, in 1238, had married Henry's sister Eleanor. Many barons were uneasy with a programme of reform which gave too much scope to his ambition. They became increasingly disunited, and in 1261 Henry recovered power.

Montfort was the only baron who refused to accept Henry's recovery of power and in 1263 became undisputed head of a revived movement for reform.

At the battle of Lewes on 14 May 1264, he won a stupendous victory against all the odds. A form of control by council was imposed on the king, and the real power lay now with Simon. However, Gilbert of Clare, the young earl of Gloucester, and Edward, the king's son, caught Simon at Evesham on 4 August 1265 and massacred him and his army. His head was cut off and his testicles hung either side of his nose.

Death of a Pious King

In 1269 the new abbey church at Westminster was consecrated and St Edward the Confessor's body was translated to its new shrine within it. Three years later, Henry died and was buried in Westminster Abbey in the very tomb from which the Confessor had been removed.

The Osney Abbey chronicler, in his epitaph to the king, noted that 'he loved aliens above all Englishmen and enriched them with inummerable gifts'. Certainly, in the patronage he gave to the Savoyards and Lusignans, Henry was at odds with the growing feeling of Englishness that was characteristic of the 13th century. Yet, unlike his Plantagenet predecessors, he lived almost entirely in England.

Six years before Henry died, the chronicler of Tewkesbury Abbey, on a false rumour of his death, penned the king's obituary, describing him as 'a lover and adorner of holy church; a protector and consoler of religious orders; a vigorous governor of the kingdom...'.

Other obituaries written and stories circulated after his death balanced Henry's piety with his simplicity. Dante placed him in purgatory as 'the simple king who sits apart'. Salimbene recounted how Henry was thrilled when a jester told him he was like Christ, only to order the jester's execution when he heard the explanation: 'concerning Christ, it is said that he was as wise at his birth as he was when he was 30. In the same way you are as wise now as you were as an infant.'

Henry III consults master masons during the construction of Westminster Abbey. The new church was consecrated in 1269, and Henry was buried there three years later.

Edward I

(1239-1307)

KING OF ENGLAND 1272-1307

'He was skilful in the conduct of affairs of state and
was from boyhood dedicated to the practice of arms'
William Rishanger

*Edward I; renowned for his
chivalry, he also had a
reputation for
untrustworthiness.*

A Martial King

Edward I was tall, with long arms and legs (hence his nickname 'Longshanks') that enabled him to wield a sword with dexterity and ride the most spirited horse. His left eyelid drooped a little, and he lisped, but he was 'effectively eloquent in speech when persuasion was necessary in business'.

Edward's changes of direction during the war between Henry III and the barons earned him a reputation for untrustworthiness even before he came to the throne; he was as capable of faithlessness as his grandfather King John.

Decisive in war, chivalrous and conventionally pious, he lavishly endowed an abbey at Vale Royal in Cheshire (but ceased to support it in 1290). His piety did not prevent him from dealing severely with the clergy and Robert Winchelsea, archbishop of Canterbury, when they crossed him over taxation in the last decade of his reign.

As king, Edward banned the tournaments in which he had taken such a prominent part in his youth – to ensure that his knights' attention did not wander from military campaigning. His interest in the chivalrous and action-packed legend of King Arthur and Camelot contrasted markedly with his father's attachment to St Edward the Confessor and his miracles.

The first two decades of his reign witnessed a great surge of governmental energy. The king started in 1274 by instigating country-wide investigations into the usurpation of royal rights and lands following the civil war of the 1260s, and into abuses by local officials.

As a result of this survey, the first statute of Westminster was enacted in parliament in 1275. Its many detailed clauses tried to deal with the abuses the investigations had revealed.

In 1285 the government attempted to improve peace-keeping by stipulating that all men over the age of 15 should hold specified arms and be ready to use them, under official direction, to maintain law and order. Two years later, in 1287, keepers of the peace were appointed in the counties to supervise this militia. However, there was no improvement in order and, on the contrary, after 1294 when war broke out with Philip IV of France over Gascony, in the prevailing atmosphere of war, lawlessness in the countryside increased. In the last decade of his reign, Edward's remarkable successes in war and government began to turn sour. His constant and voracious demands for money and men for his wars with France and, from 1296, with Scotland produced strong baronial opposition, and in 1297 the king averted a major political crisis only by abolishing the most detested tax, the 'maltote' (levied on wool).

In the four years before his death in 1307, Edward levied taxation more cautiously, and borrowed immense sums of money from Italian bankers to finance his continuing wars. His position in Scotland began to improve – by 1305 it seemed that he had finally conquered that kingdom – and in the same year a former clerk of his, Bertrand de Got, was elected pope, taking the name of Clement V. Almost immediately, in 1306, the new pontiff suspended Robert Winchelsea, archbishop of Canterbury, at that stage the king's principal opponent, from office.

Edward I was nicknamed 'Longshanks' because of his height and his long arms and legs – characteristics suggested by the artist in this contemporary portrait.

The Much-Loved Queen

Queen Eleanor of Castile was about 50 when she died of malarial complications in 1290, after a life devoted to travel and pregnancies. Blessed with an unusually happy marriage to Edward I, she had accompanied his progresses through England, France, Spain and the Holy Land, and was still travelling with him when she took to her deathbed.

In the intervals of this journeying, she had borne him 16 children, nine of whom died either at birth or in infancy. Her favourite son, Alfonso, lived only 12 years. Of the six survivors, the future Edward II had a robust constitution, which resisted his enemies' attempts to cause his 'natural' death by starvation, ill-treatment and deliberate infection. Four of the five surviving daughters died in their thirties or forties, and only Mary (a nun) lived to be as old as her mother.

Eleanor of Castile died at Harby in Lincolnshire. Her entrails were buried at Lincoln Cathedral, and her heart at the Blackfriars in London; the rest of her body was interred in Westminster Abbey. This multiple burial ensured that Eleanor's soul would have the heartfelt prayers of the Dominicans at the Blackfriars, as well as of the Benedictines at Westminster.

Edward had 12 monumental stone crosses erected to mark the 12 stages of her sad final journey from Lincoln to Westminster, only three of which, at Waltham, Northampton and Geddington, survive. These Eleanor Crosses were based on the similar 'Montjoies' which commemorated the places where St Louis's body rested on its way from Aigues-Mortes, in Provence, to its burial in St-Denis.

A floor tile in Westminster Abbey showing the three Plantagenet lions; both Eleanor and Edward I are buried in the Abbey.

Eleanor of Castile, Edward I's much-loved queen. When she died in Lincolnshire, the king erected 12 crosses to mark her final journey back to London.

Campaign in Wales

The king's first Welsh campaign in 1277 was mounted to bring Llywelyn ap Gruffyd, prince of Wales, to heel. He was disturbed by Llywelyn's marriage to Eleanor de Montfort, daughter of Simon, and also concerned by the more recent intrigues of Guy and Amaury, Simon's sons, who were still at liberty in Europe. Llywelyn was formally condemned in parliament as a rebel against the Crown. By the summer of 1277, having been deserted by his vassals, Llywelyn surrendered to the might of Edward's army.

The king seemed bent on disinheriting Llywelyn completely, but an agreement negotiated at Aberconwy allowed the prince to retain Snowdonia for his lifetime, provided he recognized the hereditary right of his younger brother Dafydd to a share of Snowdonia. Dafydd was resentful that his earlier adherence to the king was not rewarded more generously, a resentment deepened by his friction with royal officers who administered the land which bordered upon his own.

The war of 1282 was instigated by Dafydd rather than Llywelyn, who, despite his grievances, preferred more politic solutions, perhaps influenced by his wife. When Dafydd rose in rebellion at Easter 1282, Eleanor was with child, and

Caernavon Castle, one of the fortresses built by Edward I to subdue the Welsh, was a royal residence as well as a stronghold.

Llywelyn did not join him until June, when his wife died giving birth to a daughter. His active participation in the Welsh movement brought it great strength; it was late autumn before Edward was in a position to attack Snowdonia. Llywelyn, hoping to revive Welsh resistance in the south, moved to Builth, where he died in combat on 11 December 1282. His severed head was taken to the king at Rhuddlan and then displayed at the Tower of London. English chroniclers describe the derision with which it was greeted by the London crowd.

The Hammer of the Scots

In 1290, the legitimate heir to the Scottish throne, Margaret, Maid of Norway, died, and Edward was asked to arbitrate between 13 claimants. His choice, John Balliol, was unpopular, and first William Wallace, then Robert Bruce, rebelled against him. Edward I's attempts, and, later, those of his son Edward II, to gain control over Scotland gave rise to long and savage wars. The outcome turned, to a great extent, on the possession of Scotland's castles and fortified towns. At the outset of the fighting in 1296, Edward's first action was to storm the inadequately defended border town of Berwick upon Tweed, slaughtering the

The stone of Scone under the throne in Westminster Abbey. It was brought to England by Edward I's men in 1296.

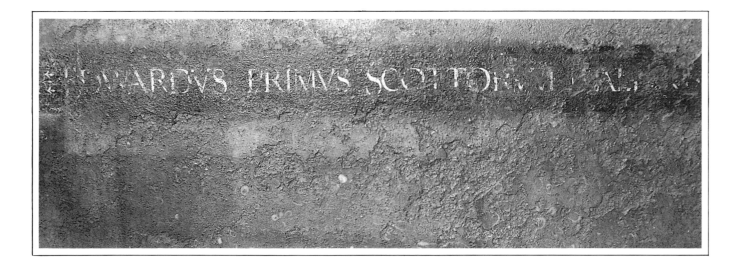

inhabitants almost to a man. Less than six months later, after over-running Scotland, he took care that all the country's fortresses should be 'stuffed with Englishmen'. By garrisoning vital strong-points like Edinburgh and Stirling, he could command the main routes through Scotland, but it soon became clear that this did not give him control over the whole nation. Instead, the English generally occupied the castles while the Scots dominated the countryside between them.

In 1296, Edward I went on a relic-collecting expedition to deprive the Scots of their regalia and spiritual treasures. His men removed what they believed to be the stone of Scone, on which the Scottish kings were enthroned, taking it to Westminster Abbey, where it lies under the throne on which English monarchs are crowned.

When the Scots temporarily gained the upper hand – as they did under William Wallace in 1297–8 – they were unable to dislodge the invaders from all their fortresses. When they did manage to acquire a castle, they were rarely able to keep it; Edward's military expertise and superior financial resources enabled him to bring all the latest refinements of siegecraft into play.

Neither side was able to achieve final victory until a new Scottish leader, Robert Bruce, emerged in 1306, and with him a new war strategy. Abandoning conventional methods, the Scots tried to starve the enemy out by applying a 'scorched earth' policy, and made all-out efforts to capture the English strongholds. Their weapons were the rope ladder and the cunning ruse – like the farmer's cart used to jam open the gates of Linlithgow. When the fortresses were taken, they were systematically reduced to rubble.

Edward died at Burgh by Sands on 7 July 1307, on his way to fight the Scots once more. One chronicler suggested that his last wish was for the flesh to be boiled away from his bones, so that they then could be carried with the army on every expedition into Scotland. Another said that he had asked for his heart to be buried in the Holy Land. But neither wish was to be fulfilled, for Edward was taken complete to Westminster Abbey, his family mausoleum, for burial. It is ironic that this king who, in his construction of lavishly decorated family tombs and memorial crosses for his wife Eleanor, had shown so marked an interest in the panoply of death, was himself laid to rest under a plain slab inscribed: 'Here lies Edward I, the hammer of the Scots'.

The inscription on Edward I's tomb; the king was known as 'the hammer of the Scots'.

Edward II

(1284-1327)

KING OF ENGLAND 1307-27

'He whom the world hated was robbed of his kingdom,
but received into the kingdom of the angels'
Geoffrey le Baker

Edward II; one of England's most unsuccessful rulers, he was ultimately deposed by his wife, Isabella of France, and murdered.

A Spendthrift King

When Edward II came to the throne in 1307 he was acclaimed by the people. He was tall, strong and handsome, and, even if his tastes were extravagant, he had fought without major mishap for his father in four Scottish campaigns, and had acted as regent during the king's absences abroad. In 1301 he had been created prince of Wales and earl of Chester, and although his father had often upbraided him for his gambling and unruliness, this kind of behaviour was not unusual among young Plantagenet princes. He was an excellent horseman – an important quality – and could on occasions appear decisive.

Yet Edward of Caernarvon proved to be one of the most unsuccessful kings ever to rule England. His excessive reliance on his male favourites – the greedy, hedonistic Piers Gaveston and later, the ambitious, grasping Hugh Despenser and his son of the same name – opened a rift of bitterness and mistrust between him and his barons which proved impossible to heal.

Concerned at the way Edward was mismanaging the affairs of state, a major coalition of barons, the Ordainers, rose in opposition to the king. In 1311 its leaders forced him to agree to a series of ordinances for the better governance of the kingdom, but its unity was destroyed when Guy de Beauchamp, 10th earl of Warwick, and Thomas, 2nd earl of Lancaster, engineered Gaveston's death in 1312. The disagreements between Edward and the barons allowed Robert Bruce to conquer large areas of Scotland. Edward led a large army north in 1314 to relieve the siege of Stirling, but was defeated by Bruce at the battle of Bannockburn.

Contemporary chroniclers were, unusually, almost united in their criticisms of the king. It was not just that he was a lazy spendthrift, so obsessed with his favourites that he was incapable of governing. He was also a failure as a military leader, and a coward, as when he fled from the battle of Bannockburn. He had no taste for traditional kingly pursuits, such as tournaments, but was addicted to eccentric activities such as hedging and ditching, cutting down trees, building walls, thatching, blacksmith's work, and rowing boats – all in the company of humbly born men: a chamber book of 1322 notes substantial payments to Robin and Simon Hod, Wat Cowherd, Robin Dyer and others for spending 14 days in the king's company.

Edward also loved to breed and race horses, play music (he had his own small orchestra) and act; indeed, it was rumoured that Walter Reynolds, royal chancellor and archbishop of Canterbury, earned preferment because of his abilities as a theatrical director. The king's tastes, in short, resembled those of a rich and irresponsible 18th-century gentleman, but to his subjects his habits were incomprehensible: rumours spread that he was a changeling and no true son of the great Edward I.

When Edward's queen, Isabella, daughter of Philip IV of France, invaded England with her lover Roger Mortimer in 1326 and deposed the king, many of his supposedly loyal subjects flocked to support them.

Edward II is created prince of Wales by his father, Edward I. He grew to be extravagant, cowardly and irresponsible.

The King's Favourites

A Gascon and the son of a knight in King Edward I's service, Piers Gaveston was brought up in the household of the king's son, the future Edward II, and attracted that feckless young man's favour to an extent which can only be described as obsessive.

On becoming king, Edward II heaped riches upon him, and made him earl of Cornwall.

The relationship between Edward and Piers was undoubtedly homosexual, as shown by contemporary chroniclers. They make several references to physical intimacy between the two men as when Edward preferred to invite Gaveston, rather than his new wife, Isabella, to share his bed.

The barons objected to Gaveston's total domination over the king, and only the favourite's death could offer a final solution. This was engineered on 19 June 1312 by the earls of Warwick and Lancaster, in dubious judicial proceedings held on Blacklow Hill between Warwick and Kenilworth. On hearing of Piers's end, the distraught king vowed that he would not be buried until he had avenged his murder. He kept Gaveston's embalmed body at the Dominican friary in Oxford for three years, but in vain. Eventually, in 1315, he laid it to rest at the Dominican friary at King's Langley, which he lavishly endowed in memory of his beloved.

Hugh Despenser and his son of the same name were Edward II's last favourites. The elder Despenser, a consistently loyal servant, was much hated by Edward's enemies for his influence over the king after Gaveston's death.

The younger Despenser, born in about 1290, was betrothed by Edward I to the sister of the young earl of Gloucester in 1306, at the age of 16. At the start of Edward II's reign in 1307 he was a landless knight who, unlike his father, joined the baronial opposition to Gaveston. The death of the earl of Gloucester at Bannockburn brought him sudden wealth and status: his wife was the heiress to one-third of her brother's vast estates.

By 1318, the younger Hugh was Edward II's undisputed favourite. Like Gaveston he was a powerful character on whom the weak king depended; unlike Gaveston, he was a vicious, utterly immoral man, whose sole purpose in life was to acquire wealth and power. Intensely arrogant, he was once heard to regret his inability to control the wind. His wealth was astonishing, and he was so proud that he had made no effort to recruit support in the kingdom.

The Despenser regime was based on fear alone and it collapsed like a pack of cards in 1326 when Queen Isabella and Roger Mortimer invaded England.

The elder Hugh was strung high on the public gallows at Bristol, vilified by the mob as a traitor. The younger Hugh Despenser was executed at Hereford.

Hugh Despenser the Younger, Edward II's favourite after Gaveston's death, was brutally executed when Isabella and Roger Mortimer invaded England in 1326.

Alabaster effigy of Hugh Despenser; during his life, his main purpose had been to acquire wealth and power by any means.

Bannockburn and After

Ordinances which greatly restricted Edward II's power were drawn up in February 1310 by the great men of England, and became law at the parliament of September 1311. They were the culmination of a series of petitions from 1307 onwards, criticizing several fundamental aspects of Edward's government, and drastically restricted the royal prerogative. Their authors, the ordainers, were the kingdom's leading aristocrats.

The ordainers' unity was destroyed, however, when two of them, the earls of Warwick and Lancaster, murdered Gaveston in 1312. Some members of the group felt that there would now be opportunities to mitigate Edward's worst excesses, and became his supporters. Lancaster, on the other hand, disagreed.

Two years later, in 1314, Edward was humiliatingly defeated at Bannockburn by Robert Bruce, whose offensive in the north in 1310 had forced the king to launch a lacklustre and poorly financed campaign in southern Scotland. Scottish counter raids followed, and Robert Bruce wrought destruction as far south as Durham, exacting protection money on the way.

By spring 1314, only five major strongholds remained to be won, including Stirling, the strategic key to Scotland. In the summer of 1313, its beleaguered captain, Sir Philip Mowbray, had bought time by promising the Scots that if they would abandon their siege immediately, he would yield it to them at midsummer 1314 – unless the English had come to his aid before then.

This shamed Edward into taking a large army into Scotland and on to the Forth Valley plain near Stirling. The force, well equipped, and well trained, consisted essentially of cavalry. The Scottish host which met it was primarily an infantry army, adequately fed and in excellent spirits after its recent run of victories. The two sides were vastly different, but in many ways they were well matched.

On 23 June, the encounter began when Henry de Bohun charged alone against Robert Bruce. Robert side-stepped the levelled lance and de Bohun collected Bruce's axe in his brains.

That evening, the English made a tactical error, abandoning their position by the roadside for a field where they were hemmed in between the River Forth and the Bannock Burn. At daybreak, the Scottish army bore down on them, schiltrons bristling with spears, and crushed them into the marshy ground. Panicking English troops tried to escape across the burn, and soon the stream was dammed with bodies.

The rout was completed by the Scottish guerillas and camp followers, who fell upon and massacred the English as they attempted to flee. Edward and his household were turned away from Stirling Castle by the pragmatic Mowbray, who fully intended to surrender to the Scots without further complications. With difficulty, Edward escaped to Dunbar, from where he took a boat, and ignominiously returned home.

A year after Bannockburn, Lancaster took control of the kingdom and forced the king to observe the ordinances once again. Surly and unprepossessing, Lancaster fell out with many of the barons, and the king soon re-asserted himself with the acquiescence of most of the great men of the realm.

Robert Bruce, victor of the battle of Bannockburn in 1214, when Edward II was defeated and forced to flee.

As a result of widespread opposition to the Despensers, however, Lancaster was able to rebuild his following and, in 1321, once again took control of the affairs of state. Edward crushed him by force when, in 1322, the royal army defeated him in a battle near Burton-on-Trent. He was taken to Pontefract, tried and condemned as a traitor.

The barons found it impossible to control Edward II for any length of time, partly because of his character, and partly because of their preconceptions about his royal office. They believed he was their divinely crowned and anointed king to whom they owed fealty, advice and support. They were not his keepers and opposition to him was an extreme and undesirable step.

Procedures like those in the ordinances ran counter to the medieval political system, and, after 1322, Edward used the possibilities inherent in this basic fact to establish a fresh and truly vicious tyranny with the Despensers' aid.

Deposition and Death

Isabella of France played a dark and momentous role in the history of England. She came to England in 1308 as a 12-year-old bride, but was overshadowed in Edward's eyes by Piers Gaveston, to whom he gave all the best jewels, rings and other wedding presents which Isabella had brought from home. When the barons engineered Gaveston's death in 1312, Isabella became closer to the king, and the future Edward III was born later that year.

However, in the 1320s, Isabella changed from Edward's relatively co-operative consort to his implacable enemy and, between 1325 and 1327, the 'she-wolf of France' skilfully organized Edward II's betrayal and destruction. In March 1325, Edward and the Despensers sent her to France to negotiate a treaty with her brother, Charles IV of France. There, with her lover Roger Mortimer, earl of Wigmore, she rallied support for her cause, and, on 24 September 1326, invaded England.

Edward II tried to rally London to his defence, but, meeting with hostility, he panicked. On 16 November the king and his handful of followers were captured near Neath by Henry, earl of Leicester. He was deposed in favour of his son Edward in January 1327 and, in April that year, was imprisoned at Berkeley Castle, Gloucestershire, where he was probably murdered by his gaolers.

Berkeley Castle, Edward II's last home. He was imprisoned there in April, 1327; in September of that year his death was announced and a funeral was held for him at Gloucester Abbey.

Carving of Isabella, 'the she-wolf of France'. She and her lover, Roger Mortimer, governed England for three years after the crowning of her son, Edward III.

Edward III

(1312-77)

KING OF ENGLAND 1327-77

'Grace and prosperity made him renowned and illustrious'
Thomas Walsingham

Edward III was a charismatic ruler whose personality and life-style emphasized the authority and splendour of the monarchy.

A Dominant Monarch

One of the dominant personalities of his age, Edward III was a man around whom legends gathered. Over six feet tall, he towered over his contemporaries literally as well as figuratively. He was above all a man of action and passion, energetic, restless, generous to a fault, a lover of display and pageantry. The swashbuckling coup by which he seized power in 1330 set the tone for his reign, and for his great feats of arms against the Scots whom he defeated at Halidon Hill in 1333, and in the battle of Crécy in 1346, nine years after the outbreak of the Hundred Years' War in 1337. He was never happier than when leading his troops on campaign, or jousting and feasting with his knightly companions in arms.

Fourteen years old when he was crowned, Edward was for three years king only in name, and remained firmly under the tutelage of his mother Queen Isabella and her lover Roger Mortimer, who had usurped royal authority.

Opposition to Mortimer was led by Henry of Lancaster with the support of the king's uncles, the earls of Norfolk and Kent, but Mortimer moved quickly to crush his enemies. The weak and foolish Edmund, earl of Kent, was the most vulnerable. He was tricked into believing that his brother Edward II was still alive and became involved in plots to secure his release. These were immediately reported to Mortimer, who accused the earl of treason and secured a conviction on his own confession.

Edward was no longer a boy, however, but a man of nearly 18, a husband and the father of a son, the future Black Prince. Since becoming king he had experienced nothing but humiliation at the hands of Isabella and Mortimer. The judicial murder of Kent gave added urgency to the plans of Edward and his well-wishers to seize power from the over-mighty Mortimer.

The trap was sprung in October 1330. Isabella and Mortimer were arrested by Edward and his men in Nottingham Castle. Isabella was firmly retired from public life at Castle Rising, while Mortimer was arrested and condemned to death. He was drawn through London to the Elms at Tyburn, and hanged.

It was Edward's good fortune to be ideally suited by physique, temperament and taste for the role to which he had been born. He was also lucky in his marriage to Queen Philippa, daughter of the count of Hainault, who bore him 12 children. Her calm good nature, gentleness and dignified tolerance of her husband's infidelities won her universal affection. After her death in 1369 Edward deteriorated rapidly into premature old age.

Edward III. During the 50 years of his reign, his court was the most magnificent in Europe and his armies the most feared.

St George's Chapel, Windsor Castle, built to house Edward III's Order of the Garter, founded in 1344.

Edward knew instinctively that political stability depended on maintaining good relations with the nobility. Successful military campaigns, tournaments and the chivalric orders of the Round Table and the Garter all strengthened the bonds between the king and his barons. His love of display and ostentation, too, was more than mere extravagance. Fine clothes, magnificent feasts and great building projects like Windsor Castle boosted the image of monarchy, emphasizing its splendour and wealth and, as a result, its authority and stability. There may have been a darker side to Edward III's passions. He was notoriously licentious, and rumours circulated about his affair with the 'countess of Salisbury', probably Alice, wife of Edward Montague, younger brother of the earl of Salisbury. The chronicler Jean le Bel relates how the king brutally raped Alice, leaving her battered, bleeding and dishonoured.

The Hundred Years War

The Hundred Years War was only the final phase of a much longer struggle, which began when William the Conqueror, duke of Normandy, became king of England in 1066. By 1250 the only substantial English possession left in France was the duchy of Aquitaine or Gascony. Edward I only narrowly defeated an attempt to confiscate and conquer Gascony in the 1290s, and it soon became clear to Edward III in the 1330s that his cousin and adversary Philip VI was looking for any excuse to repeat the attempt.

The struggle was increasingly taking on international dimensions. The Scots, fighting desperately for their independence against Edward III, found firm allies in France. For his part Edward III sought to cultivate support in the Low Countries. The final breach was caused by fear in England of a French invasion. Edward III secured a large war tax from a worried parliament, and in the following year the French made a pre-emptive strike by invading Gascony. The Hundred Years War had begun.

Edward III possessed a powerful weapon denied to his predecessors in the struggle with France: a claim to the French crown. The Capetian royal house, which had passed the French throne from father to son in unbroken line from 987, suddenly came to an end in 1328. The three sons of Philip the Fair had occupied the throne in succession and all died childless. The crown passed to their cousin (and Edward III's), Philip VI of Valois.

Edward III was Philip the Fair's grandson through his mother Isabella of France, and, in 1337, when Philip declared Gascony forfeit to the French Crown, Edward was able to trump his adversary's ace by asserting his hereditary rights. In 1340 he formally laid claim to the kingdom of France and added the fleur-de-lis to his coat of arms.

On 26 August 1346, Edward III gave battle at Crécy, in his county of Ponthieu, to a French army that had the confidence which comes from overwhelming strength. Genoese crossbowmen led the French advance, but their bowstrings were ruined by rain (the English bowmen kept theirs dry inside their helmets) and they were driven off by the English cannon.

The French cavalry then advanced into the 'valley of death' formed by the English army, riding down the Genoese who had preceded them. The hail of English arrows and the obstacles threw their attacks into confusion.

There were 15 French assaults, all pressed with the utmost bravery, but they could make no headway against such a strongly defended and narrow front. Throughout the battle the English maintained a strong discipline, and resisted the temptation to break ranks to take rich prisoners. The French finally admitted defeat and fled, leaving behind perhaps 4000 dead knights.

The battle, in which Edward's son, the Black Prince, acquitted himself with honour, was a shattering victory for tactics developed over the preceding decades, and taught the French a healthy regard for English fighting skills.

The battle of Crécy, one of Edward III's greatest triumphs, and the first of a series of English victories over the French.

A Noble Wife

Philippa, Edward III's queen, was the daughter of William count of Hainault, Holland and Zeeland. She and Edward were close in age and remained deeply attached throughout their long marriage, even though the king was not always faithful. Philippa was by no means beautiful, but she was warm-hearted, intelligent and physically hardy. She bore Edward 12 children, only three of whom died in infancy, and accompanied her husband on his campaigns.

For the first time since Henry II, the king had a large family of sons growing to manhood. However, unlike Henry's children, Edward III's sons remained on remarkably good terms with each other and, more importantly, with their father. The queen was an important moderating influence on her husband, who relied on her advice and encouragement. Deeply religious, she had a strongly developed sense of the responsibility of kingship.

Early in Edward's reign she encouraged clothworkers from her own country to settle in Norwich and train Englishmen in cloth manufacture. The experiment prospered and from cloth she turned to coal, gaining permission from the king to exploit the mines on her Tynedale estates. Coals were soon being carried south from Newcastle as well as east to the Low Countries.

Philippa's greatest failing was her extravagance; although this benefited luxury trades in London, it was less than ideal for a country financing an expensive war. Edward finally abolished her separate household.

The queen's interest and concern for ordinary people made her beloved in a way few queens have been before or since. In 1369 the chancellor, in his address to parliament, said of her, 'Behold, lords, if any Christian king, or any other ruler in the world, has had so noble and gracious a lady as wife.'

Heraldic tiles with (centre top) one showing the three Plantagenet lions. Although, like many of his family, Edward III was unfaithful to his wife, the marriage was a happy one.

The Siege of Calais

Edward's victory at Crécy in August 1346 left him free to besiege Calais at the beginning of September. Standing at the point where the Channel is narrowest, the town was a nest of pirates who preyed on English shipping, and a vital base for future attempts to conquer France.

Edward decided the only way to take Calais was to starve it out. His preparations were meticulous. From England he called for men, cannon and ships: the army of 32,000 men that he raised was the largest of his reign.

To house this multitude during the winter he erected a town of wooden buildings around a central market place, where the Flemings came to sell food twice each week.

In Paris, Philip VI trusted in Calais' strength to resist during the winter and spring. He summoned an army in March 1347 but it was not ready to march until mid-July. Although Philip claimed to be eager to fight he had no such intention. On the night of 1 August he fled.

The English king, enraged at the defenders' 11-month resistance, determined to make an example of them. The governor and six leading citizens were forced to carry the keys of Calais to Edward, barefoot and hatless, halters around their necks. It may or may not be true that Queen Philippa, a moderating influence upon her hot-tempered husband, saved them from execution when, heavily pregnant, she knelt before the king and pleaded for their lives. Certainly, the town's citizens were expelled and replaced with Englishmen, and Calais became an English colony in France for nearly two centuries.

An Inglorious Old Age

In 1360 Edward recognized the magnitude of the task he had set himself in conquering France and relinquished his claims to the country in return for undisputed title to Aquitaine. Nine years of peace followed, but hostilities with France resumed in 1369 and the English gradually lost ground.

The re-opening of the war with France in 1369 marked the beginning of the final, inglorious phase of Edward III's reign. Queen Philippa was dead, the Black Prince stricken with illness and the king himself was declining into a premature old age. Effective leadership of the kingdom passed to Edward's third son John of Gaunt, duke of Lancaster, who lacked the stature and popularity of his heroic older brother. Within a few years, despite crippling war taxes, the English had lost virtually all their French lands apart from a few strips of coastal territory. While the French advanced, the once mighty Edward III lapsed into his dotage. His physical and mental decline was symbolised by a senile infatuation for his mistress, Alice Perrers. Her power over the king was complete. Edward could deny her nothing, and she controlled access to him. England had seen royal mistresses in the past, but never one who had influenced the course of justice and the government of the kingdom.

Edward III's effigy in Westminster Abbey. The king died in 1377, a year after the 'Good Parliament'; in his old age he declined mentally and physically.

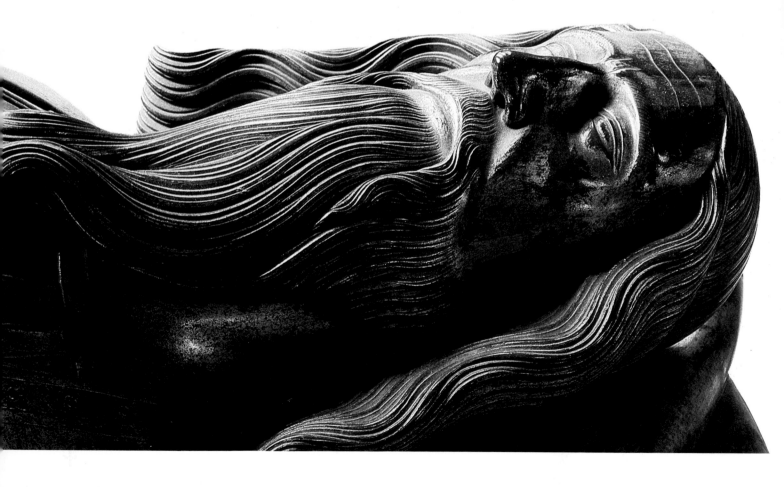

The Houses of Parliament. The 'Good Parliament' of 1376 saw the development of impeachment, based on the assumption that the king's ministers were accountable to parliament as well as to the monarch.

Widespread discontent with the failures and corruption of the king's government came to a head in the 'Good Parliament' of 1376. As soon as it opened it became clear that there were members of both houses determined to attack those who controlled the king. For the first time, the House of Commons rather than the Lords took the initiative. Members refused to make any tax grants until their grievances had been redressed, and elected Peter de la Mare to act as their spokesman: the first man to serve as Speaker of the Commons.

Its effects were short-lived: John of Gaunt was able to reverse most of its acts in the following year. Nonetheless it was of great historic importance because of the development of impeachment, which rested upon the basic assumption that the king's ministers, as public officials, were accountable not just to the king but to parliament which represented the whole community of the realm.

Like his grandfather Edward I before him, Edward III lived too long for the good of his historical reputation. In spite of his great military victories, the later years of decline cast a shadow over his triumphs in France.

Richard II

(1367-1400)

KING OF ENGLAND 1377-99

'He would talk to no one but would look at people,
and whoever he looked at, whatever his rank,
he had to genuflect'
A Eulogy of history, continuation

Richard II; intelligent and cultured, he could also be psychopathic, brutish and politically inept to an extent that had seldom been seen in medieval England.

An Inept King

Richard II, son of Edward, the Black Prince, and Joan, the Fair Maid of Kent, became king at the age of ten: his father had died in 1376, a year before the death of Richard's grandfather, Edward III. During his minority England was ruled by a council, under the guidance of John of Gaunt, 2nd duke of Lancaster, and the young king was put in the charge of Sir Simon Burley.

For all his privileges, Richard was a solitary and sad youth. With no father and no brothers, he depended on the company of women – the strong-minded Princess Joan and later his own Queen Anne. His one close friendship, with the young Robert de Vere, earl of Oxford, was ruinous to his political career.

In his isolation, Richard sought solace from the arts; surviving portraits of the king, done when he was still only in his late twenties, reveal the delicate fingers and finely chiselled features of a true connoisseur. The great tragedy and irony of Richard's life was that he combined artistic sensitivity with a political ineptitude that resulted in the Merciless Parliament and, ultimately, his own deposition and death.

His one act of political astuteness, which was not repeated, came in 1381 when he was only 14 years old. For a few short weeks in June and July, many parts of England were threatened by riots and demonstrations: the start of the Peasants' Revolt, the immediate cause of which was the poll tax, granted to the king by parliament in 1380. Every man and woman over the age of 15 was to pay a standard levy of one shilling to the crown.

The real centre of the unrest was London, where rebel bands from Essex united with men from Kent on 13 June to form a force conservatively estimated at 10,000. On 14 June, at Mile End, Richard assented verbally to the rebels' demands, buying time for their anger to cool. He retracted these concessions later, but he declared a general pardon after December that year.

Richard II addresses his rebellious subjects at Mile End, during the Peasants Revolt. His success convinced him that he was a capable leader of men.

Richard II's badge, a white hart set in enamelled silver. The king, whose court had been renowned for its luxury, died a prisoner in Pontefract Castle, Yorkshire.

John of Gaunt, Richard II's uncle; the leading member of the council that ruled during the king's minority, he tried to save him from his own foolishness.

Wives to Richard II

Anne of Bohemia and Richard II were both 15 at the time of their marriage in 1382 and the queen became an effective moderating influence on Richard, who loved her dearly; and particularly after the death of his mother in 1385, Anne provided a strong, stable core to his life. She took her role as Richard II's consort seriously. At each crisis in his reign such as the Peasants Revolt, and executions after the Merciless Parliament, she advocated moderation and reconciliation. When she died in June 1394, at the tragically young age of 27, the king was heartbroken. Deprived of Anne and isolated from his friends, Richard became increasingly irascible and unpredictable.

Two years after her death he married Isabella of Valois, the seven-year-old daughter of Charles VI of France, and grew attached to the child, who plainly adored him.

When Richard died, Isabella – then ten years old – and her household were moved to Wallingford in Berkshire while Henry IV tried to extricate himself from the embarrassing position in which her presence in England placed him. She should by rights have returned immediately to France, but this would have meant giving back her dowry and jewels. For Henry, the obvious and most satisfactory solution would have been to marry her to his heir, the future Henry V. The French, however, were opposed to an alliance with the man they believed had usurped Richard's throne, and Isabella, steadfast in her loyalty to her husband's memory, flatly refused to countenance the match. There was a prolonged dispute over her dowry, and the little queen endured two lonely years of widowhood before she was allowed home to France – at a cost to Henry of £4000.

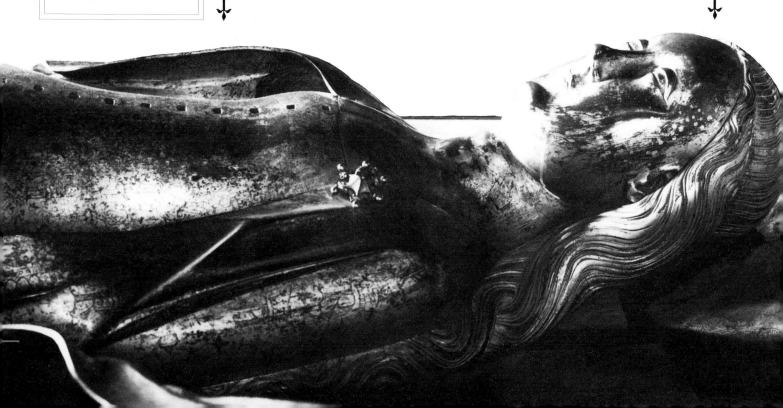

A Most Unpopular Favourite

None of Richard II's favourites was as hated or despised as Robert de Vere, ninth earl of Oxford. Born in 1362, he was five years older than Richard, with whom he spent much of his boyhood. Married to Edward III's granddaughter, Philippa de Coucy, while still a teenager, he exploited to the full his strong connections at court.

Richard's reckless generosity towards his favourite became little short of a national scandal. In creating de Vere marquis of Dublin, for example, Richard introduced a foreign title and bestowed an almost unprecedented amount of authority upon him. When the marquisate was converted into a dukedom, in 1386, rumours that Richard intended eventually to make de Vere king of Ireland seemed to be more than idle speculation.

In the long run, it was de Vere's general contempt for the aristocracy, as much as the prominent part he played in helping Richard to undermine the authority of parliament, that in 1387 led the lords who rose against Richard's tyranny – the lords appellant – to demand his execution for treason, along with four other crown servants.

Although de Vere was ready enough to take up arms, he showed little aptitude as a commander. He was trapped by the rebel lords at Radcot Bridge, Oxfordshire, in 1387 and then deserted his men by swimming the Thames under cover of fog; and after a last interview with Richard in London he fled abroad, never to return alive.

Not surprisingly, the earl was one of the first victims claimed by the Merciless Parliament of 1388. His estates and titles were confiscated, and he was sentenced in his absence to be hanged, drawn and quartered. He died, apparently in great penury, in 1392, after being savaged by a wild boar while out hunting.

Robert de Vere, earl of Oxford. In 1387 he was condemned to death by the lords appellant, but escaped to exile in France.

Courtiers dressed in the height of fashion. Royal courts were hives of political intrigue, one of the reasons why Richard II's favourites were unpopular.

A Famous Parliament

The most famous – or notorious – of the 24 parliaments which met during Richard II's reign is undoubtedly the Merciless Parliament of 1388. In it the bitter political struggle between Richard II and his advisers on the one hand, and the majority of the lords and commons on the other, was fought out.

In November 1387, Richard's uncle, the duke of Gloucester, and the earls of Warwick and Arundel had 'appealed' (accused) five of the king's closest intimates of treason. Richard was threatened with deposition and, after a feeble show of resistance, had to summon parliament.

The assembly which gathered at Westminster on 4 February 1388 was truculent, and the commons as a whole wanted a sweeping purge of the royal household. The five so-called traitors were summarily convicted; some lost their lives; others fled overseas. In early March, the commons demanded the impeachment of the judges who had endorsed Richard's attempt to undermine the authority of parliament.

Otterburn, site of a battle in 1388 in which English forces were attacked and defeated by the Scots.

New College, Oxford. Despite the upheavals of Richard II's reign, foundations like this, and Winchester School, were established by William of Wykeham, bishop of Winchester and the king's chancellor.

Many members of the upper house believed that the lords appellant threatened to outdo the king in vindictiveness. While the commons pressed for the further impeachment of Richard's confessor and four knights of his chamber, the more moderate peers believed it was time to call a halt.

Although they were successful in the short term, the lords appellant failed to impose lasting restraints upon the king. They removed his friends, and temporarily curbed his despotism by placing him under the control of a council. But their intransigence fuelled Richard's desire for revenge.

In the summer of 1388, while the English administration was in disarray, the Scots with whom there had been an uneasy peace for two years mounted a two-pronged attack against Ireland and northern England.

On 5 August, at Otterburn in Redesdale, the defending English army, under the earl of Northumberland's eldest son, Henry Hotspur, set upon and was defeated by the smaller, diversionary Scots force led by the expedition's commander, James, earl of Douglas, in a battle commemorated in one of the most famous and evocative of border ballads: 'Chevy Chase', a celebration of the Scots victory, and of the chivalric ideal.

Richard subsequently made occasional threatening overtures against Scotland, but was anxious for peace in the north. The Scots felt secure enough to deny England a peace treaty while the terms were unacceptable to them.

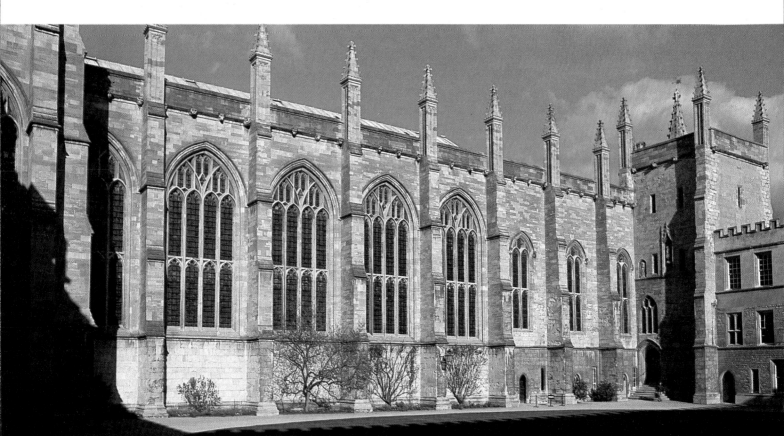

The Usurper and the King

Henry Bolingbroke, one of the five lords appellant and son of John of Gaunt, had been sent into exile in 1398. On his father's death in the following year, Richard II refused to allow the Lancastrian estates to pass to him. As Gaunt's heir, Bolingbroke found himself at the head of a growing band of the king's enemies, who had suffered similar wrongs; and in the summer of 1389, while Richard was in Ireland, Bolingbroke invaded England.

On hearing the news, Richard took ship from Waterford, landed in Wales and tried to drum up military support. Bolingbroke advanced on Chester and a deputation was sent to the king, at Conway Castle. Two of its members, the earl of Northumberland and the archbishop of Canterbury, suggested to the king

Richard II yields his crown to Henry Bolingbroke, his cousin and successor.

that he should restore Bolingbroke's Lancastrian inheritance and surrender certain of his councillors for trial. Both swore on the Host that he would then be left free to rule and Richard agreed to the terms in good faith. But when he left Conway, Northumberland was lying in wait, and the king suddenly found himself a prisoner in Flint Castle. Bolingbroke had become the effective ruler of England.

Summonses were issued in Richard's name, calling a parliament to meet at Westminster at the end of September, and the king was taken south and lodged in the Tower pending this assembly. It was by no means clear what would happen next.

Bolingbroke became increasingly impatient of constitutional arguments, and when parliament assembled he stepped forward and claimed the empty throne, having made sure there was a large body of Londoners at the doors of Westminster Hall ready to acclaim him. It was necessary only to justify the revolution by discrediting Richard's regime. Richard was declared a tyrant who had forfeited his right to rule.

He was told of his deposition on 1 October. Four weeks later he was taken from the Tower, disguised as a forester, and led to Pontefract Castle in Yorkshire. By February 1400, King Richard II was dead. Starvation is the most likely cause, though it is not clear whether this was self-inflicted or imposed on him by his jailer, Sir Thomas Swynford. His body was taken to London and buried alongside Queen Anne in the royal mausoleum at Westminster Abbey.

Henry IV was evidently anxious to quell the rumours that Richard had escaped imprisonment and death and was about to reclaim the throne. However, these stories continued for some years, and were often a cause for concern to the new Lancastrian regime. Ironically, Richard proved more popular in death than he had ever been in life.

Richard II's coat of arms from the Wilton diptych which commemorates the king's coronation.

HENRICVS ·IIII·

Henry IV

(1366-1413)

KING OF ENGLAND 1399-1413

'...raised to the throne, he followed
the paths of justice'
John Capgrave

*Henry IV, Richard II's
cousin, was admired
throughout Europe, but had
no training in kingship.*

The Troubled King

Henry Bolingbroke, duke of Lancaster, was about 33 years of age – a few months older than his cousin Richard II – when he became king in 1399. Unlike Richard, Henry of Lancaster had travelled widely, to tournaments near Calais, to a crusade against the pagans in East Prussia, and on a pilgrimage to the Holy Land by way of Venice. Recently he had been exiled in Paris.

He had won admiration throughout Europe for his 'singular virtues', including faithfulness to his wife, Mary de Bohun. Renowned as a fighting man and a jouster, Henry was also educated, literate and musical. Of stocky build, he cut an elegant and dashing figure. However, he had had no training for kingship. His invasion of England was made deceptively easy by Richard's unpopularity and his own skill as a military leader, but the crown was more easily won than held and he fought to keep it for nearly a decade.

On 12 October 1399 at the Tower of London Henry knighted some 50 young noblemen, including his own four sons, and the next morning after their vigil they rode with him to Westminster, where he was crowned with all the traditional ceremony. At the banquet that followed, the king's champion rode into the hall offering to defend him against all comers. Henry replied that he would, if necessary, defend himself, and this he soon had to do.

Although many lords and other landholders were opposed to Richard, few were wholeheartedly for Henry, who, within months of his coronation, was forced to suppress a rising planned by Richard's supporters. The new king had to learn to confront critical parliaments and open rebellion at home as well as enemies abroad. His only real supporters were the tenants of his Lancastrian estates, and the few people who found reconciliation with Richard impossible.

Henry's two main allies on his path to the throne were Thomas Arundel, whom he restored to the archbishopric of Canterbury, and Henry, earl of Northumberland, head of the Percy family. Arundel remained his lifelong councillor, but the Percys, unenthusiastic for Henry even in 1399, supported him only so long as it suited their ambitions, and from 1403 to 1408 they rose against him.

When the parliament which had deposed Richard met again as the first parliament of the new reign, it took away the titles conferred in 1397. Otherwise the revolution claimed few victims.

Both Scots and French were ready to take advantage of any English weakness. Henry decided to settle the Scots first and invaded Scotland in the autumn of 1400. He reached as far as Edinburgh, but the Scots withdrew before him and he was unable to bring them to battle. Shortage of money and provisions forced him to return to England, where he was presented with another problem: the Welsh under Owen Glendower had risen in revolt.

The French continued to observe the truce made with Richard II, but urged the return of his young widow, Isabella, who remained in Henry's hands.

To add to Henry's difficulties, parliament made him no grant beyond the usual customs duties, and the king and his council, fearful of the unpopularity that would result from taxation, did not dare to ask for funds. Shortage of money was an enduring problem throughout the reign.

An enamelled gold swan, a version of a pendant that Henry IV customarily wore. It was the device of the de Bohuns, his first wife's family.

Henry IV's effigy in Canterbury Cathedral. He had few wholehearted supporters during his reign.

The Breton Queen

In 1399 Henry IV had been a widower for five years and needed a queen to grace his court and share the loneliness of a king's life. His second wife was Joan, daughter of Charles of Navarre, widow of Duke John IV of Brittany. The marriage was never popular, but Henry was a generous and faithful husband and Joan a good wife to him.

For much of Henry V's reign, the new king was unmarried, and Joan continued to preside over her stepson's court as she had done over his father's. Henry treated her with the honour and respect he might have accorded his mother, and when he concluded a truce with Brittany in 1417 he said he had done so in response to her appeals. Nevertheless, in September 1419, when Henry V was in France, Joan was arrested on the order of her second stepson, John, duke of Bedford.

The reason given in parliament for this extraordinary action was that her confessor accused her of attempting 'the death and destruction of our lord the king'. The council had to take seriously this accusation of witchcraft made against her, but it is unlikely that many at court really believed it.

Joan was never formally charged and, after an initial imprisonment at Pevensey, lived in style and comfort in her own castle of Leeds, in Kent. Henry V ordered her release on his deathbed three years later. For the rest of her life Joan lived in affluent retirement. She died in 1437 and was buried at Canterbury with Henry IV.

Leeds Castle, home of Joan of Brittany. Accused of witchcraft, but never formally charged, she had been briefly imprisoned at Pevensey before coming to the castle.

A Welsh Hero

Descended in the direct line from the princes of Powys in North Wales, Owen Glendower had studied at the Inns of Court, but, like all his class, he was also proficient in arms: he is said to have served in Richard II's army. The occasion of his rebellion against Henry was a dispute with Lord Grey of Ruthin, an English marcher lord and a close ally of the king.

Glendower was proclaimed prince of Wales in 1400 and on 18 September he and his followers burned the town of Ruthin, the centre of his enemy's lordship, and other English settlements. But within a week a force raised from Shropshire overwhelmed his small army. By the time Henry reached Shrewsbury on 26 September the revolt seemed over and the king was able to lead his army around North Wales. Henry IV returned to Westminster, leaving his son Henry, prince of Wales, in nominal charge in North Wales with the earl of Northumberland's son, Henry Hotspur, as his chief councillor and the real commander.

Glendower and his surviving companions went into hiding, and waged a guerilla war against the English. On Good Friday 1401 Conway Castle was captured by a party of Welsh rebels while the garrison was hearing mass. In the summer Henry IV returned to Worcester with his army, determined to end the rebellion. Again, he failed to bring Glendower to battle.

In 1402, the rebels captured Lord Grey and Edmund Mortimer, the young earl of March, who by the strict rules of primogeniture was the true heir of Richard II. Henry soon arranged for Grey to ransom himself, but showed no eagerness to see Mortimer freed. The latter's sister was Hotspur's wife and in 1403 the Percys' discontent came to a head. Hotspur proclaimed his revolt, and marched on Shrewsbury. But the king arrived first, and defeated Hotspur on 21 July. Hotspur died in the battle and Worcester was executed.

The king's victory ensured the eventual downfall of Glendower as well as of the Percys. Henry, prince of Wales, now 16, slowly reconquered the country and finally drove the Welsh leader into hiding. Glendower was never captured and the obscurity of his end made him a national hero.

Henry Percy, earl of Northumberland. The Percy family conspired with Glendower against Henry IV, but was defeated by the king in 1403.

End of an Unquiet Reign

In May 1410 Henry IV named his councillors in parliament at the request of the commons. For the first time since 1399, the archbishop of Canterbury was omitted. The new list was headed by Henry, prince of Wales, freed by his own successes from the fighting in Wales. Sir Thomas Beaufort became chancellor, and other members included the bishop of Winchester (Henry Beaufort). The two Beauforts, the king's half-brothers, were the prince's closest advisors.

For some time the king had been suffering from a debilitating and disfiguring disease, and he now withdrew from London to the Midlands. The prince of Wales, with the council, was in charge of government for nearly 18 months, until in November 1411 shortage of money forced the council to summon another parliament.

The king was at Windsor when the parliament was due to meet and wrote to say that he was too ill to reach Westminster in time. This was probably the moment when Bishop Beaufort suggested that Henry IV should be persuaded to abdicate in favour of his son. Certainly, the king realized that he needed to make a great effort to keep his crown and suddenly seemed to recover his former energy. In parliament on 30 November he thanked the prince and other councillors for their services, effectively dismissing them from office.

Although mortally ill, Henry was at last triumphant. The Scots had not dared to attack since their boy king James had fallen into English hands in 1406; the Welsh rebels were defeated and the French divided between the dukes of Burgundy and Orleans with both sides seeking English help. Finally, in the last year of his reign, the prince of Wales sought reconciliation with him.

Henry died on 21 March 1413, aged about 47. The fact that he was still king almost 14 years after landing at Ravenspur, and that after an unquiet reign he was able to leave an undisputed succession to his son, is evidence of his ability and character.

A Yorkist genealogy shows the Lancastrian Henry IV cutting off Richard II's line. For many of his subjects he remained a usurper throughout his reign.

Henry V

(1387-1422)

KING OF ENGLAND 1413-22

'... pious in soul, taciturn and discreet in his speech,
far-seeing in counsel, prudent in judgement'
Thomas Walsingham

Henry V; pious and a gifted leader who united his people behind him, he was a legendary figure even in his own lifetime.

Defender of the Realm

Henry V was tall, clean-shaven and tight-lipped, sinewy and agile, more clerical than military in appearance. Determined to impress his subjects as a great king, he insisted on respect for his dignity, and any who insulted or underrated him did so at their peril.

The principal functions of a king were to defend the realm from its enemies and rule his people with justice, and in both Henry V fulfilled the ideal. He relished war, fighting in the thick of the battle at Agincourt and engaging in single combat in a mine beneath the walls of Melun. Like every good commander, he cared for his men and won their confidence; but he was also a stern disciplinarian, who executed on the spot any who disobeyed his commands. He was ready to take risks, and only superb generalship at Agincourt saved the expedition from disaster. However, the conquest of Normandy two years later was achieved by careful military and diplomatic planning, which always put him one move ahead of his adversaries. He studied the art of war and used artillery on a scale hitherto unknown.

Henry's ambitions were boundless, and infused with a sense of his destiny. He believed that he, and the English nation, had been chosen by God to humble the pride of the French, and that France and England should be joined together under his rule, bringing the Hundred Years War to an end and uniting christendom in a crusade to the Holy Land.

He had no doubts about the rights of his cause – and presented himself to his subjects as the embodiment of justice. Shortly after becoming king Henry V had accompanied the Chief Justice to the Midlands to investigate oppression. Throughout his reign, even while he was on campaign in France, humble petitioners brought their complaints to him and received royal writs ordering redress for them.

In the first years of his reign he crushed a major Lollard uprising and a conspiracy to assassinate him by nobles loyal to Richard II's memory.

The failure of both plots strengthened the king's position, for it was seen as evidence of God's protection. At the same time Henry took positive steps to win the nobility's loyalty by fair treatment and bold leadership, while his severe and disciplined piety reinvigorated orthodox religion.

Henry V also breathed new life into royal government. He brought order into the crown's finances by planning his income and expenditure and refusing to live on credit, and scrutinized officials rigorously, punishing corruption and insisting on the crown's rights and dues. As a result, he won the confidence and support of the house of commons.

The king took the initiative and set the pace in all these spheres, advised and supported by the greater nobility and bishops. In addition to his brothers he could rely on his half-uncles, Thomas Beaufort, duke of Exeter, who defended Harfleur against the French in 1416, and Henry Beaufort, bishop of Winchester, chancellor until 1417, who lent the king large sums for his campaigns. By 1417, with nobility, Church and nation united behind him, Henry V was already becoming a legend.

Henry V receives a book on kingship from its author, Thomas Hoccleve.

The score for 'Gloria' by 'Roy Henry', possibly Henry V himself. The king's victory at Agincourt was celebrated by the 'Agincourt Carol'.

The first course

Boar's meat with mustard	Eels in sauce
Frumenty with sea-bream	Pike
Pickled lampreys	Trout
Codling	Plaice
Fried merlin fish	Large crabs
Lombardy pork slices	Meat en croûte
Small pies	

A special confection

❖

The second course

Galantine	Minced chicken
Bream	Conger eels
Sole	Mullet
Chub	Barbel
Roach	Fresh salmon
Halibut	Baked gurnard
Broiled rochet	Fried smelt
Lobsters	Damascus slices
Lamprey en croûte	Royal pork pie

A special confection in the shape
of a chef and a lady

❖

The third course

Compôte of dates	Sauce of mixed herbs
Wild carp	Turbot
Tench	Perch
Gudgeons	Sturgeon, fresh and pickled
Whelks	Baked porpoise
Fried monkfish	Freshwater crayfish
Large shrimps	Baked eels and lampreys
White slices	Meat en croûte, decorated
	with four angels

A special confection in the shape of a tiger,
with St George leading it.

❖

The Widowed Queen

The menu for Catherine's coronation feast. Henry V's queen was crowned in London in February 1421, and widowed 18 months later, in August 1422.

Henry V had met Catherine, daughter of Charles VI of France and Isabella of Bavaria, briefly in 1419 and had apparently been charmed by what he saw. Chroniclers on both sides of the Channel tell of his love at first sight, but the king's later behaviour suggests that his infatuation was short-lived.

The couple were married at Troyes Cathedral in June 1420. Catherine made a state entry into London in February 1421 and was crowned by Henry Chichele, archbishop of Canterbury. Before the king returned to France they were sure that Catherine was pregnant, and she remained behind in England to await the birth of their child. The future Henry VI was born at Windsor on 6 December 1421 and early in the New Year Catherine travelled back to France. She was staying with her parents at Senlis at the time of her husband's death in 1422, and accompanied his body back to England, a widow at 21.

With so young a widowed queen, the question of remarriage raised all kinds of problems. The suggestion that Catherine was contemplating marriage to her late husband's cousin, Edmund Beaufort, prompted parliament to pass a statute in 1428 prohibiting anyone from marrying a queen dowager without the express permission of the king – given only after he had reached the age of discretion. Catherine was not prepared to wait until her son grew up and in about 1429 she married an obscure Welsh squire, Owen Tudor, grandfather of the future Henry VII.

A betrothal feast in honour of a bride. Although Henry V was captivated by Catherine when he first met her, his infatuation did not last.

A Famous Victory

Agincourt, the greatest battle of Henry V's reign and one that resounds through English history, took place on 25 October 1415. The 5,000 to 6,000 English, forming a single dismounted line, faced some 50,000 to 60,000 French. Like the English, the French were on foot, but with squadrons of armoured cavalry on each flank, ready to ride down the archers.

The battle of Agincourt; Henry V's victory was a moral and strategic triumph that paved the way for further successes in France.

The French remained stationary for nearly three hours and Henry eventually advanced first, halting within bowshot to shower the enemy with arrows. This provoked a disastrous French cavalry charge. The victorious English took many high-ranking prisoners at this stage. However, when a new French assault threatened, Henry ordered his men to slay prisoners of lesser rank, lest they turn on their captors. A half-hearted new attack by the French materialized, but was swiftly turned into a wholesale flight: the English had won the battle of Agincourt.

Henry's English subjects celebrated with great rejoicing, and he returned to England in November, and made a triumphant entry into London.

In 1416 Henry allied with the emperor-elect Sigismund, king of Germany, and the house of Burgundy, preparatory to another French campaign. War was renewed in 1417, and Henry, profiting from divisions between the Burgundian and Armagnac (Orleanist) camps, had by 1419 reached Paris. He had captured Normandy, and much of Picardy and the Ile-de-France, starving out the city of Rouen by a long siege (1418-19).

In May 1420, by the Treaty of Troyes and shortly before his marriage to Catherine, Henry was adopted as heir to her father Charles VI of France.

Back in France by June, after a brief visit to England with his new queen, Henry advanced south of Paris to the Loire, attempting to bring the dauphin to battle. By October he had settled down to besiege Meaux, the key to Champagne. The city finally capitulated in May 1422. It was the king's last triumph: he had contracted dysentery and by the end of August lay dying in the castle at Vincennes. His final commands were to confer the government of France on the elder of his two brothers, John, duke of Bedford, and to commit to the younger, Humphrey, duke of Gloucester, the guardianship of his son and heir, still less than a year old.

Henry had restored the crown to its full dignity and authority after the calamities of the 14th century. He governed his subjects with justice and mercy and strove to extend his empire over France, the ancient enemy, to bring peace and security to both realms. Although all this was achieved in a remarkably short time, much remained to be done when he died and his death left the English in an untenable position in France.

Henry V's effigy in Westminster Abbey. He died of dysentery a few months after capturing the town of Meaux.

Henry VI

(1421-71)

KING OF ENGLAND 1422-61, 1470-71

'... neither intelligent enough nor experienced enough
to manage such a kingdom as England'
Jean de Waurin

*Henry VI; the only
Plantagenet monarch never to
campaign against a foreign
enemy, his reign saw the start
of the Wars of the Roses that
divided England for more
than 30 years.*

A Peace-Loving King

Henry VI was barely nine months old when his father, Henry V, died, and was 16 years old when he officially assumed his royal powers in November 1437. He had begun to take a positive role in government a year before that. There is no sign that he was not physically and mentally up to the task of kingship. He was good-looking, intelligent and sharp – every inch a king. As a young man, he enjoyed hunting, gaming and spending money on fine hats and gowns. After his death, he was remembered as being tall, slim and well proportioned; when his tomb was opened in 1910 the bones were those of a 'fairly strong man' of about 50, Henry's age at death.

A strong character rather than formal education made a successful king in the Middle Ages. Emotionally, Henry was naïve even before the mental collapse in 1453 that triggered off the Wars of the Roses that devastated England from 1455 to 1487. Despite the distinguished soldiers in his household, he developed no martial instincts, and was the first English monarch never to command an army against a foreign foe: the English gradually lost ground in France during his reign as the French captured Brittany in 1449, Normandy in 1450, and the historic English possession of Gascony in 1453. By that time all England's former French territories save Calais had been lost.

Lectern effigy of Henry VI in King's College Chapel, Cambridge. The college was founded by the king in 1440.

Richard Beauchamp, earl of Warwick; he tutored the young king in knightly accomplishments: 'good manners, letters, languages...'

Sensieut vnst petit traittie dentre
lame deuote z le cuer lcgl sappelle le
mortissiement de vaine plaisance fait
z compose p rrne roy de seale duc darou
p luy made z intitule a tresreuered
pere en dieu larcheuesq de toure
lcgl traittie fu fait en lan ssil·iiij·
lb·Et dugl comence le proesme·

Tresreuerend pere en dieu se
han par la duunc grace ar

A Political Queen

The daughter of René, duke of Anjou, self-styled king of Sicily, Naples and Hungary, and a niece by marriage of Charles VII of France, Margaret was a fitting bride for Henry VI, even without a dowry. Although her father was rich only in titles and talents, the marriage in 1445 was a symbol of peace between England and France. There was optimism that a permanent peace would follow. Margaret had been brought up in Italy and was learned as well as beautiful. She was 16 at the time of her marriage. Henry was 23 and, as a papal envoy observed, he was more like a monk than a king and avoided the company of women. Nevertheless, the marriage seems to have been at least averagely happy; the couple chose to spend much of their time together. For eight years Margaret was childless, a major dereliction of queenly duty – and politically crucial, for Henry had no close heir presumptive. When she finally gave birth to Edward, prince of Wales, in 1453, her husband had lapsed into mental illness and was unable to recognize his infant son.

Margaret came from a family which for several generations had relied for political survival on the determination and resources of its womenfolk and she instinctively took up her husband's burden. But she had never learned that in England, unlike France, the crown was expected to be above faction. Politically partisan and vindictive, her lack of political judgement and moderation was one of the reasons for the fall of the house of Lancaster.

Margaret fought for her husband's cause from the outbreak of the Wars of the Roses in 1455 until 1470 when she was imprisoned by Edward IV after Henry's death. In 1475, her cousin Louis XI ransomed her for £10,000. The French king granted her a small pension on her father's death. Margaret retired to a small château near Saumur in Anjou, where she died in obscurity in 1482.

René, duke of Anjou, in his study. His daughter Margaret, Henry VI's queen, was strong-willed, learned and beautiful.

Profile portrait medallion of Margaret of Anjou. She was childless for eight years before giving birth to Edward, prince of Wales.

The Wars of the Roses

The weak link in Henry VI's genetic chain came from the Valois. His maternal grandfather, Charles VI of France, had been subject to fits of insanity. In August 1453 Henry VI fell into a trance-like condition which affected him periodically for the rest of his life.

There were three possible contenders for the regency that became necessary: Henry's wife Margaret, and his cousins Edmund Beaufort, duke of Somerset,

and Richard, duke of York, who was eventually created protector and defender of the realm in March 1454. He fulfilled this office with integrity and industry. But at Christmas 1454 the king regained his senses and the regency was no longer required. York faced a future in the political wilderness unless he took up arms to preserve the place he had held in the king's council.

Ironically, it was thus not Henry's madness but the recovery of his sanity which made the Wars of the Roses inevitable.

When the Lancastrians regained power, York and his friends were excluded from their former government offices, and, expecting that worse would follow, they withdrew northwards and began mustering men. Their apprehensions were confirmed when Somerset called them to a 'great council' at Leicester. The Yorkists marched south in full force, to encounter the royal party at St Albans on 22 May 1455.

Victory went to the Yorkists, who also gained control over Henry – the duke became protector once more. The king had not put on armour, and was slightly wounded in the neck by an arrow. There was no question of deposing him: the king retained the loyalty of the whole nation, including most nobles, who as yet favoured neither the 'Red Rose', Lancastrian party nor the 'White Rose' Yorkist party but were simply anxious for a peaceful settlement.

The king also wanted peace and, even after the close of York's 'second protectorate' in February 1456, tried to remain on good terms with the duke. But Margaret, 'being a manly woman, used to rule and not be ruled', sought revenge, and set about creating a new Lancastrian party. She moved the seat of government from London (strongly Yorkist in sympathy) to the West Midland Lancastrian estates. Within less than two years Lancastrians and Yorkists were again at war; and so well did the king's supporters succeed that by the end of 1459 York and his major adherents were all in exile.

Between July 1460 and March 1461 there were three violent changes in political fortunes in England and no less than five battles were fought on English soil. Executions of captured nobles added to the bloodshed, which reached a climax with the struggle at Towton, one of the bloodiest engagements in the wars. The first of the battles was at Northampton in July 1460. The result was the capture of Henry and the reassertion of Yorkist control.

Exile and Death

Wakefield Bridge, site of the battle in December 1460 in which Richard, duke of York, Henry's rival for the English throne, was killed.

Until early in 1461, the fortunes of both parties to the civil war swung back and forth. Richard duke of York was killed and his eldest son Edward became the Yorkist leader. King Henry, like a piece of baggage, changed hands between the rival armies. When the Yorkists could no longer claim to be ruling in the name of Henry VI and the interests of the realm, they were forced to proclaim Edward king. Their aim now was to depose Henry. Margaret, the driving force behind the Lancastrian cause, was supported by the majority of English nobles who had taken up arms. To deal with this Lancastrian threat, Edward carefully gathered an exceptionally large army as he moved north during March.

Battle was not long delayed. On 29 March the two armies, each numbering about 50,000 men, met at Towton on the road from Pontefract to York. The battle ended in victory for Edward although the greatest prizes eluded him: Margaret fled to Scotland with her husband and son, where she was joined by the dukes of Somerset and Exeter and other Lancastrian nobles.

After Edward IV's accession in 1461, Henry spent four years as an exile in Scotland or a fugitive in northern England, until he was seized in Lancashire in 1465 and taken, bound to his saddle, to the Tower of London where he was imprisoned for five years. He was restored to the throne in October 1470, after Warwick's invasion. The king was deposed for the second time early in 1471 when Edward IV returned from exile, and was returned to the Tower where he died, probably murdered, on the very night that the victorious Edward of York reached London (21 May).

Eagle badge of Richard, duke of York. Although he died in 1460, and Henry 11 years later in 1471, the struggle between Yorkists and Lancastrians continued until 1487.

Edward IV

(1442-83)

KING OF ENGLAND 1461-70, 1471-83

'... a Catholic of the truest faith and a most stern enemy
of heretics, a most benevolent patron of learned men'
Dominic Mancini

*Edward IV, a descendant of
Edward III, was the first of
England's two Yorkist rulers;
he reigned for 22 years.*

An Extravagant King

Edward was six feet three inches tall and of a big build, handsome, affable and accessible; the first son of Richard, duke of York, Henry VI's lieutenant-general in France, he had a claim to the throne as a descendant of Edward III through both the male and female lines.

Although he had no pretensions to scholarship or to more than conventional piety, he was not a philistine and took much of his library with him on his travels. His court circle included some notable patrons of learning, like George Neville, archbishop of York, but his own literary tastes were mainstream, and his extensive building schemes were mainly secular rather than religious in emphasis. Even St George's chapel at Windsor, which he reconstructed magnificently at great expense as a royal mausoleum, was intended as much to glorify the house of York as to 'serve Almighty God'.

Edward could be charming. In 1475 the Milanese ambassador described how his London neighbours – hard men of business – were elated to have talked to him and had given him the money he had asked for. But contemporaries were above all struck by his extravagance, laziness and love of luxury. His expenditure on items such as 'chambers of plesaunce' with rich hangings, on personal finery, exotic food and jewels was prodigious; on one occasion he reputedly offered as much as £3,000 for a huge ornament decorated with diamonds and rubies. He was also licentious and debauched; even Sir Thomas More, in his otherwise flattering portrait of the king, wrote that 'he was of youth greatly given to fleshly wantonness'. The names of two of his mistresses are well known. Elizabeth Lucy was the daughter of Thomas Wayte, a member of the minor Hampshire gentry. The affair lasted several years, from about the time of Edward's accession to his marriage in 1464. Their son, Arthur, was brought up at his father's court; in 1472 the king's tailor was ordered to provide clothes for 'my lord the bastard'.

The best documented was Elizabeth (more commonly known as Jane) Shore. Her father was a wealthy London merchant named Lambert and she married the goldsmith William Shore. Sir Thomas More writes that when she became the king's 'merry harlot', her husband put her aside; certainly she had her marriage annulled in 1476 on the grounds of her husband's impotency. The king took especial pleasure in Jane, 'for many he had, but her he loved'.

Edward's pursuit of pleasure often distracted him from the cares of state. De Commynes commented that his preoccupation with hunting, coupled with over-confidence, allowed the Lancastrians to recover power in 1470-1.

This crisis did, however, bring out energy and determination in Edward. As a military commander he showed himself confident and decisive; as a ruler he began to seem more ruthless and determined. In his later years despotic tendencies and an increasing lack of political grasp underlay the charming façade. Behind the smiles there was a carelessness that was not attractive to everyone – the Paston family, for instance, when the king turned a blind eye to the injustices done to them by the dukes of Suffolk and Norfolk. A lightweight as a man and as a king, Edward never discarded his childish addiction to the superficial.

Edward IV with his queen, Elizabeth Woodville, and the young Prince Edward, accepting a book from his brother-in-law, Earl Rivers.

Jane Shore, one of Edward IV's mistresses. Thomas More, clearly entranced by her, described her as fair, with a proper wit and merry in company.

Power Politics

Edward IV generally adopted a pragmatic and tolerant attitude to the nobility and tried to win them over into his service through promises of patronage and advancement. He was only partly successful. Some nobles refused to be seduced from their old loyalties to the house of Lancaster, while others – like his brother George, duke of Clarence, and the rapacious Neville clan – were so overweeningly ambitious that they turned traitor against him.

Edward relied upon an inner circle of about a dozen lords for help in government; he harnessed their ambition for high office by bolstering their authority in the regions where he employed them as his lieutenants. William, Lord Hastings, acquired unrivalled influence in the Midlands, and Sir William Herbert, earl of Pembroke, was unchallenged in South Wales. The Nevilles were dominant along the Scottish border, and Sir Humphrey Stafford, earl of Devon, in the south-west. This delicate balance of conflicting interests and personalities was seriously upset by the king's marriage, in 1464, to Elizabeth Woodville.

The daughter of Richard Woodville (later Earl Rivers) and Jacquetta of Luxembourg, widow of Henry V's brother, John, duke of Bedford, she had in 1452 married Sir John Grey, by whom she had two sons. Her husband was killed at St Albans in 1461, fighting for the Lancastrians.

For a king of England to marry one of his own subjects – and one who was a widow five years his senior – was impolitic and Edward's council took the view

Statue of Richard Neville, earl of Warwick, on a tomb. One of England's most powerful nobles, he was nicknamed 'the kingmaker'. Originally a supporter of the house of York, he later turned against Edward IV.

Warkworth Castle, seat of the Percy family. In 1470 Edward IV appointed Henry Percy, earl of Northumberland and a former Lancastrian supporter, warden of the eastern marches and restored his earldom which had been forfeited after the battle of Towton in 1461.

'that she was not his match, however good and however fair she might be and he must know well that she was no wife for a prince such as himself'.

Elizabeth was certainly fair, but although she may have been virtuous she was not good in any real sense of the word. Not very affluent, and highly ambitious, the Woodvilles – five brothers and seven unmarried sisters – and the two sons of Elizabeth's first marriage, were mainly provided for by a series of highly advantageous marriages.

The failure, in 1471, of the Nevilles and their fellow-conspirators to restore Henry VI permanently to the throne and their defeat by the Yorkists at the battle of Barnet created a power vacuum in the north, and Edward altered his strategy there as a result, during the second half of his reign. However, when he restored the Percys, in the person of Henry, earl of Northumberland, who had been imprisoned as a Lancastrian supporter, to their former authority on the East March and accorded almost vice-regal powers to his brother Richard, duke of Gloucester, he replaced the Nevilles with two 'over-mighty subjects' on an even grander and more impressive scale. He followed a similar policy in Lancashire and Cheshire, with the Stanleys, and in Wales, with the Woodvilles; in each case he consciously and deliberately increased his dependence on a small but immensely powerful clique of nobles.

Edward therefore achieved a degree of political stability during his last years, but it was bought at the expense of his authority in the regions.

Peace with France

The ending of the Hundred Years War in 1453 had made little difference to the traditional enmity between England and France and Edward began to build up a great anti-French coalition as soon as he was back on the throne. In 1474, he persuaded Charles the Bold of Burgundy to join with him in carving up the kingdom of France.

Such an ambitious scheme demanded considerable financial outlay, and for three years Edward struggled to get the English parliament to support his enterprise. The lords and commons were unimpressed, but eventually provided Edward with the £180,000 he needed to finance his campaign. The king assembled the largest army taken to France in the 15th century: 11,500 fighting men and almost as many non-combatants.

The campaign was a non-event. Edward marched south via Agincourt to Péronne, but made no move to fight. He and Louis XI met at Picquigny near Amiens. Security was tight, and the talks were conducted through a trellis to avoid assassination attempts. As in a modern summit conference, the heads of state paraded while the administrators worked. The result, the treaty of Picquigny of 29 August 1475, brought Edward considerable diplomatic and financial benefits, and kept the peace between England and France until the last year of his reign.

Carving depicting the meeting, at Picquigny, between Edward IV and Louis XI of France. Talks were conducted through a trellis to avoid assassination attempts.

An Uncertain Future

Although Edward died on 9 April 1483, a mass was mistakenly sung for his soul three days earlier, in York, probably because his final illness took the form of a death-like paralysis or coma. He was buried with proper ceremony at Windsor on 20 April.

In the relatively stable conditions of the reign, government had made a recovery. The king's approach was pragmatic; he raised new men to high offices and he put much energy into supervising routine functionings of the royal administration. An inner group of officials emerged who handled Edward's finances directly, largely by circumventing the cumbersome machinery of the exchequer, and by treating public revenues as if they were his private finances. Much of the money raised went on schemes of personal and dynastic aggrandizement – the king's attempts to arrange suitable marriages for his children were a long-standing preoccupation. England's commercial interests concerned him, but largely for the revenues he reaped from them; and the strong emphasis he laid on law and order aimed to benefit crown rather than people. Edward had restored the prestige of monarchy and had provided strong leadership, but he had created a personal regime which would be stable only as long as he survived.

In April 1483 the English people therefore faced an uncertain future.

Edward IV's great seal. A strong and charismatic ruler, he brought stability to his country – a stability that was threatened by his death.

RICARDVS · III · ANG · REX ·

Richard III

(1452-85)

KING OF ENGLAND 1483-85

'Although his days were short, they were ended with
no lamentation from his groaning subjects'
John Rous

*Richard III; widely regarded
as an evil usurper, he was
more probably a pragmatist
who believed that the end
justified the means.*

The Enigmatic King

The youngest son of Richard, duke of York, and Cecily Neville, Richard III was created duke of Gloucester at the coronation of his brother Edward IV. The heart of his power was in the north, and even after his accession he relied increasingly upon men from that region. When he married Anne Neville early in 1472 the great north country estates of the Nevilles that Anne inherited provided Richard with a power base from which he was able to launch his successful bid for the throne.

Richard's position as the king's brother allowed him to exploit royal influence on behalf of himself and his supporters, but he undoubtedly inspired considerable loyalty among his servants – loyalty which, in some cases, lasted beyond his death and is unlikely to have been entirely self-interested. Richard fulfilled contemporary expectation of a 'good lord'. He was in a position to be generous to his followers, and willing to be open-handed, both as duke and king. He upheld justice and brought peace and stability to the north.

Richard enjoyed power and understood its demands. He also resented attempts to reduce it, and this resentment was probably one of the factors behind his coup of 1483. His seizure of power also reveals his preference for immediate, straightforward solutions to problems – which could result in actions of cynical brutality. He believed that the end justified the means, and his perception of himself as the best ruler to succeed his brother led to the central paradox of his reign: that a king committed to good government could so dramatically flout the conventions of acceptable political behaviour.

In appearance Richard, unlike his brothers, apparently favoured his father's side of the family rather than his mother's. Contemporary references suggest that he was relatively short and slight; portraits show him with dark hair. His best-known characteristic, a hunch back, seems to have been a later literary invention, perhaps based on memories of a real, but slight, physical defect such as round shoulders.

The Death of the Princes

When Edward IV died on 9 April 1483, his elder son was 12 years old and the king's demise raised the question of where power should lie during the prince's adolescence. The two men with the strongest claim to authority during a minority were away from court when the king died. Richard, duke of Gloucester, Edward's only surviving brother, was in Yorkshire; and the queen's eldest brother, Anthony Woodville, Earl Rivers, was at Ludlow with the prince of Wales, whose governor he was. Power therefore rested with the royal council, which started to organize the immediate coronation of the young Prince Edward. On 24 April 1483, before a formal coronation could take place. Richard seized the young king, arrested Earl Rivers, overthrew the Woodville party, and named

Gloucester Cathedral. Although Richard III was created duke of Gloucester at his brother's coronation, his power base was in the north of England.

himself protector. Edward IV's widow Elizabeth Woodville took sanctuary in Westminster Abbey with her younger son, Richard, 5th duke of York. On 13 June Richard took Lord Hastings, a leading member of the council who had backed his coup but now feared his ambition, and had him put to death: Earl Rivers was executed ten days later on 23 June. Edward V was taken to the Tower of London and, at Richard's behest, Thomas Bourchier, archbishop of Canterbury, persuaded Elizabeth Woodville to relinquish Richard, duke of York, who joined his brother in the Tower. The legitimacy of both children was called into question by an assembly of the realm, and on 26 June Richard took the throne in his nephew's place.

In October 1483 a major rebellion led by Henry Stafford, duke of Buckingham, broke out and was promptly crushed by Richard. Buckingham was executed, and opposition to Richard focused on Henry Tudor, and was strengthened by rumours that he had arranged the murder of Edward V and his brother Richard of York in the Tower. It has been suggested that by killing his nephews Richard hoped to cut the ground from under his opponents' feet; and the choice of Henry Tudor, a political nonentity, as rival candidate sugests how nearly he succeeded.

However, the full story of the princes' death is unlikely ever to be known.

A Tudor Victory

Early in June 1485 Richard III made his base at Nottingham, in the centre of England, to await Henry Tudor's invasion with some eagerness: a decisive victory would give him the security he needed to establish his regime on a sounder footing. It was 11 August before he received word that Henry had landed near Milford Haven on 7 August turning north into England near Shrewsbury.

The two armies met near Market Bosworth in Leicestershire on 22 August; the exact site of the battle is uncertain. Although Richard's army was almost certainly the larger, its morale was low. All previous opposition had been characterized by the defection of trusted royal allies, and Richard and his men must have been expecting further betrayals – even without an anonymous message left outside the duke of Norfolk's tent warning that the king was 'bought and sold'. Some of the men summoned to the king's army had already joined Henry Tudor, others had simply not turned up. The earl of Northumberland had been Richard's loyal ally in the north-east during Edward's reign, where he must have hoped for increased influence. The north, however, was crucial to the king's power and the earl's influence was, if anything, declining. No doubt Northumberland hoped that Henry Tudor would give him a better role. His decision deprived the king of some of his most committed support.

But the *coup de grâce* was administered by the Stanleys. In 1483 they had supported Richard against Buckingham, but the relationship had subsequently cooled, and by the summer of 1485 Richard mistrusted them profoundly. He had kept Lord Stanley's heir George with the royal army, a precaution which seems to have deterred Thomas, Lord Stanley, from joining the battle. Instead, the family's forces were led by Thomas's brother William, who appears to have held aloof until the climax of the battle, when Richard and his bodyguard were committed to the charge against the troops around Henry Tudor. Stanley then threw in his men on Henry's side. The intervention was decisive; Richard's forces were overwhelmed and the king was hacked to death. His body, stripped naked, was taken to Leicester, where it was buried in the Franciscan friary.

Signature of Henry Tudor, a descendant of John of Gaunt and leader of the Lancastrian party. As Henry VII he became England's first Tudor monarch.

Bibliography

Allmand, C., *Henry V*, London, 1968

Allmand, C., *The Hundred Years War*, Cambridge, 1988

Appleby, J. T., *Henry II, the Vanquished King*, London, 1962

Bagley, J. J., *Margaret of Anjou, Queen of England*, London 1948

Baker, D., ed., *Medieval Women*, Oxford, 1978

Barber, R. W., *The Knight and Chivalry*, London, 1970

Barber, R., *Henry Plantagenet, a Biography*, London, 1964

Barlow, F., *The English Church, 1066-1154*, London, 1979

Barlow, F., *The Feudal Kingdom of England, 1042-1216*, 3rd edn., London, 1972

Barrow, G. W. S., *Robert Bruce and the Community of the Realm of Scotland*, Edinburgh, 1976

Bates, D., *Normandy before 1066*, London, 1982

Bennett, J. M., *The Battle of Bosworth*, Gloucester, 1985

Bloch, M., *Feudal Society*, trans. Manyon, L. A., 2nd edn., London, 1962

Borenius, T., *St Thomas of Canterbury in Art*, London, 1932

Brooke, C. N. L., *From Alfred to Henry III, 871-1272*, London, 1961

Brown, R. A., *The Normans and the Norman Conquest*, London 1969

Brundage, J., *Richard Lion Heart*, New York, 1973

Burne, A. H., *The Agincourt War*, London, 1956

Burne, A. H., *The Crécy War*, London, 1955

Cheney, C. R., *From Becket to Langton: English Church Government, 1170-1213*, Manchester, 1956

Chrimes, S. B., *Henry VII*, London, 1977

Clanchy, M. T., *England and its Rulers, 1066-1272*, London, 1983

Clanchy, M. T., *From Memory to Written Record, England, 1066-1307*, London, 1979

Clapham, A. W., *English Romanesque Architecture after the Conquest*, Oxford, 1934

Clarke, B., *Mental illness in earlier Britain*, Cardiff, 1975

Cox, J. C., *The Royal Forests of Medieval England*, London, 1905

Cronne, H. A., *The Reign of Stephen, Anarchy in England, 1135-54*, London, 1970

Davis, R. H. C., *King Stephen*, London, 1977

Davis, R. H. C., *The Normans and their Myth*, London, 1976

Dobson, R. B., ed., *The Peasants' Revolt of 1381*, 2nd ed., London, 1981

Duby, G., *The Chivalrous Society*, ed. and trans. Postan, C., London 1977

Duggan, A., *Devil's Brood: The Angevin Family*, London, 1957

Duncan, A. A. M., *Scotland: the Making of the Nation*, Edinburgh, 1975

English Romanesque Art, 1066-1200 (Exhibition catalogue), London, 1984

Evans, J., ed., *The Flowering of the Middle Ages*, London, 1966

Eyton, R. W., *The Court, Household and Itinerary of Henry II*, London, 1878

Fowler, K. A., ed., *The Hundred Years War*, London 1971

Fowler, K. A., *The Age of Plantagenet and Valois*, London, 1967

Frankl, P., *Gothic Architecture*, London, 1962

Fryde, N., *The Tyranny and Fall of Edward II*, London, 1979

Gibson, M., *Lanfranc of Bec*, Oxford, 1978

Gillingham, J., *Richard the Lionheart*, London, 1978

Gillingham, J., *The Angevin Empire*, London, 1984

Goodman, A., *The Loyal Conspiracy: the Lords Appellant under Richard II*, London, 1971

Goodman, A., *The Wars of the Roses*, London, 1981

Griffiths, R. A., *The Reign of King Henry VI*, London, 1981

Hall, H., *Court Life under the Plantagenets*, London, 1890

Hallam, E. M., *Chronicles of the Age of Chivalry*, London, 1987

Hallam, E. M., *Chronicles of the Wars of the Roses*, London, 1988

Hallam, E. M., *Capetian France, 987-1328*, London, 1980

Hallam, E. M., *Domesday Book through Nine Centuries*, London, 1986

Hallam, E. M., ed., *The Plantagenet Chronicles*, London, 1986

Hardy, T. D., *The Itinerary of John, King of England*, London, 1829

Harris, G. L., ed., *Henry V: the practice of kingship*, Oxford, 1985

Harvey, J. H., *Cathedrals of England and Wales*, London, 1974

Harvey, J. H., *The Plantagenets*, London, 1948

Hayter, W., *William of Wykeham, Patron of the Arts*, London, 1970

Hewitt, H. J., *The Organisation of War under Edward III*, Manchester, 1966

Hibbert, C., *Agincourt*, London, 1968

Hinde, T., ed., *The Domesday Book*, London and Markham, Ont., 1985

Holmes, G., *The Good Parliament*, Oxford, 1975

Holt, J. C., *King John*, London, 1963

Holt, J. C., *Magna Carta*, Cambridge, 1965

Holt, J. C., *Robin Hood*, London, 1982

Holt, J. C., *The Northerners*, Oxford, 1961

Horrox, R., ed., *Richard III and the North*, University of Hull, 1986

Jacob, E. F., *Henry V and the Invasion of France*, London, 1947

Johnson, P., and Leslie, S., eds., *The Miracles of King Henry VI*, Cambridge, 1923

Keen, M. H., *England in the Later Middle Ages*, London, 1972

Kelly, A., *Eleanor of Aquitaine and her Courts of Love*, London, 1952

Kibler, W. W., ed., *Eleanor of Aquitaine, Patron and Politician*, Austin, 1977

Kidson, P., Murray, P., and Honour, H., *A History of English Architecture*, London, 1967

Kightly, C. S., *Strongholds of the Realm*, London, 1979

Kirby, J. L., *Henry IV of England*, London, 1970

Knowles, D., *The Religious Orders in England*, vol. 1, Cambridge, 1971

Knowles, M. D., *The Monastic Order in England, 940-1216*, 2nd edn., Cambridge, 1966

Labarge, M. W., *Gascony, England's First Colony*, London, 1980

Landon, L., *The Itinerary of Richard I*, Pipe Roll Society, 1935

Lloyd, J. E., *A History of Wales, from the earliest times to the Edwardian Conquest*, 3rd edn., London, 1939

Lloyd, J. E., *Owen Glendower*, Oxford, 1931

Lodge, E. C., *Gascony under English Rule*, London 1926

Maddicott, J. R., *Thomas of Lancaster*, Oxford, 1970

McFarlane, K. B., *Lancastrian Kings and Lollard Knights*, Oxford, 1972

McNiven, P., *Heresy and Politics in the Reign of Henry IV*, Woodbridge, 1987

Moore, O. H., *The Young King Henry Plantagenet, 1155-83*, Columbus, Ohio, 1925

Morris, J. E., *The Welsh Wars of Edward I*, Oxford, 1901

Newhall, R. A., *The English Conquest of Normandy, 1416-1424*, London, repr., 1971

Nicholson, R., *Scotland: the Later Middle Ages*, Edinburgh, 1974

Norgate, K., *England under the Angevin Kings*, 2 vols, London, 1887

Norgate, K., *John Lackland*, London, 1902

Norgate, K., *Richard the Lionheart*, London, 1924

Orme, N., *From Childhood to Chivalry*, London, 1984

Otway-Ruthven, A. J., *A History of Medieval Ireland*, 2nd edn., London, 1980

Packe, M., *King Edward III*, London, 1983

Painter, S., *The Reign of King John*, Baltimore, 1949

Painter, S., *William Marshall*, Baltimore, 1933

Parsons, J. C., *The Court and Household of Eleanor of Castile*, Toronto, 1977

Pernoud, R., *Eleanor of Aquitaine*, London, 1967

Perroy, E., *The Hundred Years War*, 1951

Platt, C., *The English Medieval Town*, London, 1976

Pollard, A. J., *The Wars of the Roses*, London, 1988

Poole, A. L., *From Domesday Book to Magna Carta*, 2nd edn., Oxford, 1955

Power, E., *Medieval Women*, Cambridge, 1975

Powicke, F. M., *King Henry III and the Lord Edward*, 2 vols, Oxford, 1947

Powicke, F. M., *The Loss of Normandy*, 2nd edn., Manchester, 1961

Prestwich, M. C., *The Three Edwards*, London, 1980

Prestwich, M. C., *War, Politics and Finance under Edward I*, London, 1972

Pullar, P., *Consuming Passions*, 2nd edn., London, 1972

Ramsay, J. H., *The Angevin Empire, 1154-1216*, London, 1903

Richardson, H. G., *The English Jewry under the Angevin Kings*, London, 1960

Robertston, J. C., *Becket, Archbishop of Canterbury. A Biography*, London, 1859

Ross, C., *Edward IV*, London, 1974

Ross, C., *Richard III*, London, 1981

Ross, C., *The Wars of the Roses*, London, 1976

Roth, C., *A History of the Jews in England*, Oxford, 1964

Saltmarsh, J., *King Henry VI and the Royal Foundations*, Cambridge, 1972

Saul, N., *The Batsford Companion to Medieval England*, London, 1983

Savage, A., ed. and trans., *The Anglo-Saxon Chronicles*, London, 1983

Scolfield, C. L., *The Life and Reign of Edward IV*, London, 1923, repr., 1967

Smith, L. M., ed., *The Making of Britain: the Middle Ages*, London, 1985

Southern, R. W., *St Anselm and his Biographer*, Cambridge, 1963

Southern, R. W., *The Making of the Middle Ages*, London, 1953

Steel, A., *Richard II*, Cambridge, 1941

Stenton, D. M., *English Society in the Early Middle Ages*, London, 1951

Stones E. L. G., and Simpson, G. G., *Edward I and the Throne of Scotland, 1290-1296*, 2 vols, Oxford, 1979

Stones E. L. G., *Edward I*, Oxford, 1968

Storey, R. L., *The End of the House of Lancaster*, London, 1966, repr., Gloucester, 1986

Strayer, J. R., *The Reign of Philip the Fair*, Princeton, 1980

Thorpe, L., ed., *The History of the Kings of Britain by Geoffrey of Monmouth*, Harmondsworth, 1966

Tierney, B., *The Crisis of Church and State, 1050-1300*, New York, 1964

Tout, T. F., *The Place of Edward II in English History*, 2nd ed., Manchester, 1936

Tuck, A., *Crown and Nobility, 1272-1461*, London, 1986

Tuck, A., *Richard II and the English Nobility*, London, 1973

Vale, J., *Edward III and Chivalry*, Woodbridge, 1982

Warren, W. L., *Henry II*, London, 1973

Warren, W. L., *King John*, London, 1961

White, L. T., *Medieval Technology and Social Change*, Oxford, 1962

Williams, G. A., *Medieval London from Commune to Capital*, London, 1963

Wilson, A., *Food and Drink in Britain*, 3rd edn., London, 1984

Young C. R., *The Royal Forests of Medieval England*, Leicester, 1979

Index

Page numbers in *italic* refer to captions to illustrations

Acknowledgements

Barnaby's Picture Library, London: 99. The Beaufort Collection, Badminton: 103b. Bibliothèque Nationale, Paris: 47, 48, 65t; 84; 95; 125; 134. Bibliothèque Royale Albert 1er, Brussels: 132. Bodleian Library, Oxford: 29; 59; 107. British Library, London: 2; 8; 11t, b; 15; 16; 18; 20; 24; 27b; 30; 42; 45; 49; 54; 58; 83; 103t; 110; 119; 123t, b; 135; 137; 148; 151; 153. British Museum, London: 56; 96; 115t. Conway Library, London: 61; 69. Corpus Christi College, Oxford: 22. Jean Dieuzaide, Toulouse: 67r. Edimages/Caubone, Paris: 97. Sonia Halliday: 62. Michael Holford: 19. Lambeth Palace Library, London: 126; 141t. Mansell Collection, London: 32; 36; 46. Marianne Majerus: 6; 12; 23; 27t; 28; 33; 35; 38/39; 41; 50; 51; 52; 53; 57; 60; 65b; 66; 68; 70; 74; 75; 76; 78; 79; 80; 85; 87; 88; 89; 90; 92; 93; 98; 105; 108; 109; 115b; 116; 117; 118; 127; 130; 131; 136; 141b; 142; 143; 144; 149; 150; 152. Musée des Beaux-Arts, Troyes: 102. Musée Condé, Chantilly: 104. National Gallery, London: 111. National Museum, Wales: 77. National Portrait Gallery, London: 120; 128; 138; 146. Public Record Office, London: 14; 73; 145. Royal Collections Department (reproduced by gracious permission of Her Majesty the Queen): 112. Society of Antiquaries, London: 67 1. Sothebys, London: 37. Victoria and Albert Museum, London: 133. Westminster Abbey, London: 100.

DATE DUE

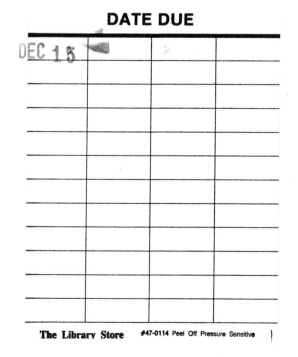

DEC 15			